AWARDS
OF THE
GEORGE CROSS

AWARDS
OF THE
GEORGE CROSS
1940–2009

by

John Frayn Turner

Pen & Sword
MILITARY

First published in Great Britain in 2006
and reprinted in this format in 2010
Pen & Sword Military
an imprint of
Pen & Sword Books Ltd
47 Church Street
Barnsley
South Yorkshire S70 2AS

ISBN 9 78184884 200 7

A CIP catalc   1 the British

All rights re   roduced or
transmitted ii   r mechanical
including phot   n storage and
retrieval syst(r in writing.

Ph(ire

Printed and bound in England by CPI

Pen & Sword Books Ltd incorporates the Imprints of Pen & Sword
Aviation, Pen & Sword Maritime, Pen & Sword Military, Wharncliffe
Local History, Pen & Sword Select, Pen & Sword Military Classics
and Leo Cooper.

FOR A COMPLETE LIST OF PEN & SWORD TITLES
PLEASE CONTACT
PEN & SWORD BOOKS LIMITED
47 Church Street, Barnsley, South Yorkshire, S70 2AS, England
E-mail: enquiries@pen-and-sword.co.uk
Website: www.pen-and-sword.co.uk

Contents

Acknowledgements

The human material for this book has come from a complex series of sources, assembled over a prolonged period of years.

First of all, I would like to acknowledge the original George Cross citations from the *London Gazette*. I have also had help over the years from the Library of the Imperial War Museum; the Victoria Cross and George Cross Association and Research Project; the Ministry of Defence; Her Majesty's Stationery Office; the files of the late Canon William Lummis, MC; the files of *The Times* and other papers; and, not least, help from *The Register of the George Cross* (published by This England Books), which has enabled me to double-check certain names and dates. I am also indebted to my publishing manager, Brigadier Henry Wilson, and diligent editor, Susan Econicoff.

Finally, I have referred to two of my own books for details of some of the classic cases of mine and bomb disposal: *Service Most Silent* described the Royal Navy's fight against enemy mines, and *Highly Explosive* included the men who were awarded the George Cross for dealing with unexploded bombs.

I would like to dedicate this book to all 160 direct winners of the George Cross.

J.F.T

Foreword

The George Cross award is the non-combatant equivalent of the VC. Early in the Second World War, King George VI was deeply impressed by the heroic deeds of servicemen in mine and bomb disposal. These were followed by comparable civilian acts connected with the war. So in September 1940 the King instituted the George Cross 'for gallantry' away from the heat of actual battle. It was to be awarded equally to service and civilian personnel, both men and women.

As the war developed, awards continued to be made for similar acts as earlier, but the range of deeds steadily widened. Non-combatant gallantry was recognized in all the services – Royal Navy, Army, and Royal Air Force, as well as in Commonwealth services.

In April 1942, there was announced the unprecedented award of the George Cross to the entire population of the island of Malta 'to honour her brave people'. This was followed later by acknowledging the supreme gallantry of members of the Special Operations Executive dropped into Occupied Europe. A number of these were posthumous awards. Accidents and disasters accounted for awards to numerous civilians during and after the war.

Awards continued to be made embracing gallantry in non-combatant areas, from the Korean War right up to the present day. The two most recent were to the Royal Ulster Constabulary as a whole in 1999, and to a soldier serving in Iraq during 2003.

A total of 160 have been made in the sixty-nine years since 1940: roughly one-third to civilians and two-thirds to service personnel. Whether in uniform or not, each one has fully deserved those two words inscribed on the silver cross 'For Gallantry'.

There is also an appendix to this book listing the names of 244 recipients of the Empire Gallantry, Albert, and Edward Medals eligible to have these converted to the George Cross.

George Cross
Recipients

Alderson, Thomas
Ansari, Matreen
Armitage, Robert
Axon, John
Bailey, Eric
Banks, Arthur
Beaton, James
Benner, Michael
Blaney, Michael
Broadfoot, David
Bywater, Richard
Charlton, Wilson
Clements, John
Cradock, Frederick
Danckwerts, Peter
Davies, Frederick
Dinwoodie, Hubert
Donoghue, Raymond
Duncan, Charles
Durrani, Mahmood
Easton, Jack
Emanuel, Errol

Andrews, Wallace
Archer, Bertram
Awang anak Rawang
Babington, John
Bamford, John
Barefoot, Herbert
Beckett, John
Biggs, Kenneth
Bridge, John
Brooke-Smith, Francis
Campbell, Alexander
Clarke, Donald
Copperwheat, Dennis
Croucher, Matthew
Davies, Robert
Dolphin, Albert
Dowland, John
Duppa-Miller, John
Eastman, William
Ellingworth, Reginald
Errington, Harry
Fasson, Francis

Fairfax, Frederick
Finney, Christopher
Foster, William
Fraser, John
Gidden, Ernest
Gimbert, Benjamin
Goad, Roger
Goodman, George
Gravell, Karl
Gray, Roderick
Guthrie, Stewart
Harris, Roy
Harrison, Leonard
Henderson, George
Hiscock, William
Horsfield, Kenneth
Hudson, Murray
Inayat-Khan, Noor
Islam-ud-Din
Johnson, Barry
Kelly, Thomas
Kennedy, James
Latutin, Simmon
Madden, Horace
Martin, Cyril
Matthews, Lionel
Miles, Leonard
Mosedale, William
Mould, John
Munnelly, Michael
Newgass, Harold
Nicholls, Arthur
Oakes, Wallace
Osborne, Albert
Patton, John
Pugh, Herbert
Rahman, Abdul
Ram, Kirpa

Ford, Douglas
Fox, Leslie
Gibson, Michael
Gillett, Ivor
Gledhill, Anthony
Goldsworthy, Leon
Gosse, George
Gray, Hector
Grazier, Colin
Hardy, Benjamin
Harrison, Barbara
Heming, Albert
Hendry, James
Hollowday, Vivian
Howard, Charles
Hughes, Joseph
Inwood, George
Jephson-Jones, Robert
Jones, Ralph
Kempster, Andre
Kinne, Derek
Lewin, Raymond
Malta, Island of
Mason, Dudley
Merriman, Arthur
Moore, Richard
Moss, Brandon
Moxey, Eric
Nairac, Robert
Newnham, Lanceray
Nightall, James
Norton, Peter
O'Leary, Patrick
Parish, Graham
Pratt, Michael
Quinton, John
Ram, Ditto
Reed, Henry

Rennie, John
Rogers, Jonathan
Ross, Arthur
Royal Ulster Constabulary
Ryan, Richard
Scully, James
Silk, Joseph
Smith, Anthony
Southwell, Bennett
Spooner, Kenneth
Stronach, George
Subramanian
Szabo, Violette
Taylor, Robert
Thompson, Jenkin
Tunna, Norman
Walker, Carl
Willetts, Michael
Wylie, George
Young, St. John

Richardson, Gerald
Rogerson, Sidney
Rowlands, John
Russell, David
Sansom, Odette
Seagrim, Hugh
Sinclair, Laurence
Smith, Kenneth
Spillett, Brian
Stevens, Henry
Styles, Stephen
Syme, Hugh
Taylor, George
Taylor, William
Tuckwell, Stephen
Turner, Geoffrey
Waters, Terence
Woodbridge, Stanley
Wright, Mark
Yeo-Thomas, Forest

Chapter One

1940

Flight Lieutenant John Noel Dowland AND
Leonard Henry Harrison,
CIVILIAN ARMAMENT INSTRUCTOR, RAF MANBY

Although the George Cross was not instituted until September 1940, these actions dated back to February 1940 and represented the first to earn the honour.

Saving a ship must be one of the most valuable acts it is possible to perform. Flight Lieutenant Dowland did this not once, but twice. Each occasion dated back to 1940, although the award was not announced until nearly a year later.

The first time Dowland had to undertake a ship-saving action was on 11 February 1940. Two enemy bombs scored hits on the grain-carrying steamship *Kildare*. One exploded in the cereal, resulting in a heavy list to the vessel. The second bomb did not go off, but remained lethally active. Worse than this, it was wedged with its nose penetrating the main deck of the *Kildare*.

In this position, the bomb was not only extremely difficult to inspect, but naturally even more inaccessible and hazardous to handle. In this condition, the captain had no choice but to edge cautiously into the Lincolnshire port of Immingham. Dowland and Civilian Armament Instructor Harrison at once boarded the ship to assess the overall conditions.

In company with another civilian instructor, the two men went into the cabin as best they could. *Kildare* crew members had

1

somehow squeezed ship's mattresses beneath the bomb, so that it would be less likely to move and thus jolt any mechanism. By good fortune, the fuses to be tackled seemed to be facing upwards – toward the rent in the penetrated decking.

Harrison had already committed to paper a proper procedure for handling these fuses, so was able to put it into practice with the aid of Dowland and the second assistant. Although it appeared routine, they knew the danger of instantaneous death. All went well, however. The locking and locating rings and the fuses all submitted pacifically. With the bomb in this state they supervised its lowering over the *Kildare*'s side and into an RAF lorry waiting by the quayside.

The same 'exceptional danger and difficulty' attended a second bomb which the Harrison/Dowland team were called on to tackle, later in the year. Another enemy bomb had hit its mark but failed to go off as intended. The bomb had lodged aboard a fishing trawler, actually attacked in the Humber estuary.

The team sent to defuse the bomb did the same thing all over again, promptly and with little fuss. Although neither of the two vessels could be described as major ships in the overall war at sea, the actions were still unique of their kind and especially memorable. Tragically, Dowland (as Wing Commander) met his death on Malta early in 1942 just over a year after the award of the George Cross to both Harrison and himself. Their actions represented the earliest to merit the GC.

Second Lieutenant Wallace Launcelot Andrews,
ROYAL ENGINEERS

As the Battle of Britain was approaching its historic zenith, on 26 August 1940 Second Lieutenant Andrews was in charge of Nos. 233 and 23 Bomb Disposal Sections, Royal Engineers. During an enemy attack on Croydon aerodrome, one bomb fell on Crohamhurst golf course but did not explode. Although it was not a danger to life, Andrews received orders to take his team there urgently and attempt to extract the fuse of the bomb for forwarding to the Director of Scientific Research. This group needed to study the fuse mechanism and take any appropriate action for the future.

While engaged on the early stages of this precarious task, Andrews began to encounter some difficulty. After he had managed to withdraw the fuse about one-and-a-half inches, it suddenly dropped back into position - actuated by what appeared to be either magnetism or a spring. He tried again and again to remove the recalcitrant component. Andrews then decided it was time to place the rest of his section under cover and proceed on his own. This would at least minimize possible casualties.

Andrews decided to improvise by tying a piece of cord to the ring of the fuse discharger. He did this with consummate care, not knowing what might happen from then on. Only a little way off from the bomb, he risked pulling on the cord to try to release the fuse mechanism.

The bomb exploded.

Fortunately, Andrews was not killed, but the blast blew him a considerable distance. Two of the men in his section were also affected by the wave of erupting air. They received splinter wounds from fragments of the bomb as it sprayed its metallic residue around the little bomb disposal team. As the later citation recognized, 'Throughout, Second Lieutenant Andrews displayed great coolness and keenness in the interests of the service.'

The scale of the increasing enemy air onslaught could be gauged by the fact that, on the very next day, another officer had to deal with two more unexploded bombs. The outcome was more tragic . . .

Squadron Leader Eric Lawrence Moxey,
RAF VOLUNTEER RESERVE

On 27 August 1940, a report reached the Air Ministry that two unexploded bombs lay embedded in the much-attacked RAF fighter station of Biggin Hill. Squadron Leader Moxey was a technical intelligence officer in London when the report came through. Within moments he volunteered to hurry from the capital to the airfield to try to render safe both bombs and then arrange for their removal.

By his technical background, Moxey was especially aware of the risks entailed in such an operation. He had, in fact, already undertaken similar jobs successfully, with utter disregard for his safety. This time, though, one of the two bombs must have been in an even more unstable state than usual. As Moxey tackled his self-imposed task, the weapon went off to its full effect. There was no hope of survival for Moxey. He had done his ultimate duty.

Aircraftman Vivian Hollowday

One night in July 1940, when returning to RAF Cranfield, Aircraftman Hollowday saw an aircraft crash and catch fire. He hurried in the direction of the flames and the wrecked aircraft. The burning debris had been scattered over a wide area by the force of the impact. Despite the chaotic scene confronting him, Hollowday found the pilot, whose clothing was by then on fire. The aircraftman put out these flames using his bare hands alone. He did not know at the time that the pilot had been killed instantly by the impact of the crash. If the flier had still been alive, Hollowday's action would have conserved his life.

By a strange coincidence, during the following month of August, Hollowday was once more returning to camp at Cranfield when an aircraft based there suddenly spun to the ground and exploded. As he ran over to the crash scene, a second explosion set up blast waves. Ammunition from the aircraft was detonating all the time, but despite the danger Hollowday snatched a gas mask from a colleague, wrapped two sacks over himself, and went into the flames.

The plane had carried three aircrew and Hollowday made four separate rescue attempts before he succeeded in releasing the first of them. He then re-entered the inferno of wreckage and again successfully got another crew member out. Tragically, however, both fliers were already dead - as was the third member of the crew.

Aircraftman Hollowday displayed amazing courage and initiative on both of these fatal occasions, Meanwhile, they represented only a comparative detail of the war in the air being flown and fought several miles overhead. After the war, Hollowday was on the committee of the VC and GC Association for twenty years.

Lieutenant Bertram Stuart Trevelyan Archer

It would clearly be repetitious to record every single bomb disposal incident in their entirety but, equally, one or two demand to be described in detail to convey the incredible courage of the men concerned.

The German deluge from the skies started in June 1940, soon after Dunkirk. But it was on 29 August that the storm began to burst over London. A mere forty-eight hours later there were 2,500 unexploded bombs waiting to be tackled. The arrival of the delayed-action fuse in enemy bombs meant that some eighty hours had to elapse before any action could be contemplated – unless circumstances were exceptional.

Right on top of the discovery of the delayed-action fuse, moreover, came the news that a type 17 clockwork fuse had been recovered with a device attached to make it explode on withdrawal – and kill all Bomb Disposal men within range. So all such fuses in future had to be removed by remote control. The War Office order for this procedure followed a famous – or infamous – incident at Swansea on 2 September 1940.

9 a.m: Lieutenant Archer received a massage to take his section from Cardiff to Swansea, where unexploded bombs were hampering efforts to control a fire at Anglo-Iranian's Llandarcy oil refinery. They saw the leaping flames as well as the smoke when they were still fifteen miles from the refinery and, as they got nearer to it, the staggering spectacle suggested that they would not be able to do much work in such fiery conditions.

10 a.m: when they arrived, however, they were met by the officer of the local Bomb Disposal section, already at work there. He guided Archer to an entry in the storage area of the refinery,

with an array of gasometer-like tanks in rows. Some were already alight, while others, though still intact, were fiercely hot.

Archer was exceedingly experienced, having dealt with some 200 bombs over the previous two or three months. In one part of this storage area, four unexploded bombs lay lurking. One had penetrated to a position directly beneath an unignited tank; another was some 150 yards away, between two tanks also still unlit and the remaining pair reposed at a safer distance from the stored oil, if safer was a word that could ever describe a bomb yet to explode. The primary object was to prevent further fires from breaking out, so Archer decided to deal first with the bomb under the tank.

Conditions could not conceivably have been worse. Fifty yards away in one direction and eighty yards in another, oil tanks were afire. The heat generated by their burning grew greater all the time. As the flames at the tops worked their way down, they melted the steel walls – so that the tanks flared like gigantic Roman candles. Smoke and flames mingled and whirled up hundreds of feet into the Welsh air, darkening the daylight yet lighting the area with their unsteady glare.

The bomb had torn its way diagonally into the concrete plinth at the base of the tank and the heat there became so intense that Archer and his support team could only work for short spells at a time. They dug in relays, working as strenuously as they could to reach the bomb before it either exploded or the tank above caught fire.

At midday, the bomb 150 yards away detonated. They all threw themselves flat. None of them was struck. No further fires were started. At 2 p.m. as they started to uncover the bombcase, one of the other two bombs went off. This stirred them to greater efforts, and soon afterwards they uncovered their own bomb completely.

It was a 250-kilogram variety, whose casing had split, leaving the main explosive filling exposed and clearly visible through the rupture. It possessed only one fuse pocket and the fuse boss had been ripped away, disclosing a tangle of wires and other confusing electrical components.

Archer decided that if he was to stop a major explosion, he

would have to remove the base plate at the rear end of the bomb – and then scoop out the main filling, which was powdered. He picked up his hammer and chisel and slowly turned the heavy base plate on its threads. Eventually it came off, and he could see that the fuse pocket was more or less loose inside the bomb.

By sheer manual force, he tore the tube free with its dangling wires and removed it from the bomb. The oil tank was now safe for practical purposes. His men could empty the filling into sandbags before carting it and the bomb case away.

The time was now 2.50 p.m. The operation had taken over four-and-a-half hours. All that while, Archer and his men must have been conscious that it was unlikely they would live to see the job finished. As well as the heat and the extra hazard of one of the adjacent tanks exploding, they had been constantly choked and confused by smoke.

Archer left his section to complete the removal of the bomb while he retired to examine the fuse pocket. He gripped the exposed wires with pliers and pulled hard until the fuse came away, revealing the clockwork delayed-action apparatus at the rear. He unscrewed the gaine, and put the electric clockwork components in his pocket. Then he peered into the tube again. There was something more than he had expected to find. He shook the tube gently, and another mechanism with another gaine slid into view.

He had hardly unscrewed this second gaine before there was a crack and a flash. A small cap inside had detonated. Archer returned to his station at Cardiff, and on reaching his billet he placed the clockwork fuse on a shelf. At 6.05 p.m. it functioned and its percussion cap exploded. He then dispatched it to the War Office, together with the other device he had found.

Later examination proved that this mechanism was in fact an anti-withdrawal device, so that if the first gaine were removed the second one would detonate, killing disposal experts.

One of the amazing things about this Swansea episode was Archer's luck. The very dangerously situated bomb he had to tackle was, unlike two others from the same stick, not timed to explode until after the period he had spent immunizing it. Forced to treat the fuse pocket apparatus very roughly, he first

7

wrenched it bodily from its cracked welding and then pulled it apart with pliers. Quite primitive.

He withdrew a fuse from above the anti-withdrawal booby trap, and was thus the first man to do so and live. He then unscrewed the gaine without doing more damage than cause a flash, so strangely delayed that the device was already separated and harmless by the time it occurred. No-one would deny that Archer deserved the George Cross awarded to him the following year – the citation quoting especially this epic episode at Swansea.

Albert Ernest Dolphin,
PORTER

Two hundred thousand bombs and two million incendiaries were dropped during the Blitz on Britain. Apart from the main assault on London, all our ports and arms towns were attacked – many repeatedly - and 43,667 people were killed. On 7 September, the RAF were a week and a day from the climax of the Battle of Britain. On this day Germany made the mistake of switching their blanket bombing of RAF bases to mass attacks on London and later on Britain as a whole. And this date has come to mark the start of the Blitz on Britain.

Saturday 7 September was a gloriously fine afternoon. The siren sounded at 4.56 p.m. A great rash of black dots was seen in the sky, moving up the Thames from the east. At 5 p.m. a fire officer saw them from his Dulwich garden; he changed his clothes and hurried to his HQ. Explosions threw up columns of smoke, growing like trees and merging into a forest of fire.

Planes came over in waves: 375 of them. They dropped loads of bombs on Woolwich Arsenal, the gasworks at Beckton, Millwall, Limehouse and Rotherhithe docks, on the Surrey docks and those by Tower Bridge, and on the West Ham power station.

The docks blazed for miles on both banks of the Thames. The sun itself seemed pale beside the crimson glare. By 6 p.m. the raiders had gone. But by 8.10 p.m. the night force appeared, guided by the fires. There were barrage balloons, but as yet no barrage. One fireman said: 'We took our pumps to East India

Docks. The fire was so huge that we could do little more than make a feeble attempt to put it out. The whole warehouse was an inferno. A large cargo ship caught fire but we put this out in half an hour. We returned to the warehouse, unable to take cover when the bombs fell. By 7 a.m. I was hunched half-asleep across the nozzle.' Firemen fought from near their engines and also from river boats.

There were nine conflagrations; sixty large fires; and 1,000 lesser ones. Thousands of houses were destroyed or damaged, factories and railways were struck and three rail termini were put out of use. Fires still burned within shells of buildings along the Thames: 430 people were killed by collapsing buildings, direct impact of bombs, or from fatal javelins of splintered glass.

It was against this backdrop of the first night of the Blitz that Albert Dolphin won the George Cross. A high explosive bomb fell on the kitchens of Ward Block I at the South Eastern Hospital in New Cross. The hospital stood not too far from the main railway lines leading to and from London Bridge Station.

The immediate casualties were four nurses in the ground-floor kitchen at the time - all killed instantly. In the adjoining ward the blast also injured the night sister and some patients. At the same time, another nurse in the ward kitchen on the first floor was hurled through the collapsing floor into the passage of the floor below.

Together with other helpers, Albert Dolphin, one of the porters at the hospital, rushed to the site of the explosion and found a nurse trapped painfully by a block of masonry across her legs. While they were working to try to release her, they heard the wall crack ominously. They had time to leap clear before the wall crumbled into a mound of masonry.

Dolphin, however, did not jump but stayed where he was, shielding the trapped nurse. His body was subsequently found by rescuers lying face downwards across the nurse, with his head towards the collapsed wall. When discovered, he had already died, but the nurse was still alive. She had sustained severe injuries, yet the rescuers were able to extricate her carefully from the rubble. Dolphin must have been aware that the wall would collapse in seconds, yet he remained where he was, throwing himself instinctively in front of the nurse in an endeavour to protect her. He saved her life at the cost of his own.

Dr Arthur Douglas Merriman,
EXPERIMENTAL OFFICER

With the sudden scattering of unexploded bombs around London and the other parts of England, neither the Air Ministry (for the Royal Air Force) nor the War Office (for the Army) were fully prepared for dealing with them. They called on the aid of the Directorate of Scientific Research, Dr Merriman offered to tackle bomb disposal jobs. He was actually graded as a civilian experimental officer, but he was probably better qualified than most people to undertake such risky ventures. It was a measure of his technical skill that he survived the summer of 1940. With the launch by the Luftwaffe of the Blitz, within four days an unexploded bomb had fallen in the heart of the capital's densely-populated West End. The date: 11 September. The location: Regent Street, the famous curving thoroughfare linking Piccadilly Circus with the crossroads of Oxford Circus.

Merriman and his Director General of Scientific Research made the brief journey from their offices at the Ministry of Supply to the spot. Needless to say, all traffic had come to a standstill. There was to be a variation in the already all too familiar clocks whirring and bombs and mines ticking. The bomb did commence to tick. They knew it would almost certainly erupt. They then decided that it was their duty to extract the explosive, or as much as they could, before anything further occurred.

With their scientific background, they had some idea how long this might be but it was really based on wishful thinking. So they pressed on as fast as they could, to get rid of the explosive. They tried to balance the probability of the bomb blowing up against the quantity of explosive remaining. As soon as they felt that the residual charge was sufficiently small they stopped and retreated rapidly. They had estimated the timing of the ticking either cleverly or luckily. After they were both safe the fuse did activate and the bomb blew up. But it had only a comparatively limited amount of explosive left in it, so instead of Regent Street sustaining heavy damage to property, morale and traffic flow, the blast merely resulted in broken glass. London was destined to survive heavier damage from the enemy over the ensuing months . . .

Temporary Lieutenant Robert Davies,
ROYAL ENGINEERS
Sapper George Cameron Wylie,
ROYAL ENGINEERS

On the very next night after the Regent Street bomb, another one fell and failed to explode in the vicinity of St Paul's Cathedral. The night of 12 September was marked by a heavy tonnage of bombs on the capital. Temporary Lieutenant Davies was the officer in charge of the Bomb Disposal Section detailed to recover the bomb, while Sapper Wylie was a member of his team.

Every incident involving unexploded bombs was fraught with maximum danger for the men responsible for rendering it, or them, safe. But in this case, Davies, Wylie and the entire team had the additional awareness that the Cathedral must be in imminent danger too, if an explosion occurred. This knowledge was accompanied by the fact that the building represented a symbol of survival and freedom for Britain.

Davies ignored thought of personal risk and spared neither himself nor his small band of Sappers in the initial efforts to locate the bomb. Wylie was, in fact, the first man to discover the weapon, deep under the pavement in front of St Paul's. They could tell that they could be killed at any second during the delicate operations to ensure its safety and removal for disposal elsewhere.

They dedicated themselves to extricating the ominously-shaped bomb, withdrawing its potentially lethal 'fangs' and making it ready for removal from this historic site, within damaging distance of St Paul's itself. Having got it out of its embedded position, they assessed the situation. The officer decided to shield his men from further potential hazard. Once the bomb had been loaded onto a waiting Army vehicle, he himself drove it away and personally carried out the disposal drill at a prearranged place. St Paul's continued to stand as a defiant symbol.

Thomas Alderson,
DETACHMENT LEADER, RESCUE PARTIES

15 September 1940. In the south, the Battle of Britain had reached its climacteric. Further north, the Luftwaffe made a number of bombing raids on the peaceful town of Bridlington, on the Yorkshire coast. Among other dwellings, a pair of semi-detached houses were totally destroyed. The falling masonry trapped one woman alive. Thomas Alderson was the detachment leader of an ARP (Air Raid Precautions) Party. He tunnelled under the unsafe brickwork to reach and rescue the poor woman. She suffered no further injury than that sustained by the original burial beneath the masonry. That was enough.

This first rescue transpired to be merely the beginning of Alderson's achievements. Some days later, two five-storey buildings were utterly demolished, and debris penetrated into a cellar, trapping eleven people there. One section of cellar had given way altogether, actually burying six of those trapped under heavy debris.

This did not deter Alderson. He tunnelled thirteen feet under the main heap of wreckage and struggled on for three-and-a-half hours in terribly cramped conditions. He became badly bruised on his way down towards the cellar. Leading the tunnelling, Alderson expected further falls at each inch of the route, as the wreckage shifted regularly, restlessly, in a dangerous fashion. Coal gas leaks made matters even more nightmarish, while fractured water pipes presented the possibility of flooding and drowning.

Through all this, and the continued presence of enemy aircraft overhead, Alderson dug down with his bare hands to reach and then release all those trapped. These two acts might have been enough to justify the George Cross for Thomas Alderson. However, the three-in-one hero still had another act to perform.

On this third occasion, five people lay trapped, once more in a cellar. An enemy air attack had shattered the four-storey building. Alderson again led the rescue drive. He helped to excavate a tunnel from the pavement of the road, through the foundations of the tall buildings, to the actual cellar. He then personally tunnelled many feet towards the cellar where the people were trapped. A three-storey-high wall above him swayed in a gusty wind. All the rescuers realized that it must be only a matter of time before this wall fell on them.

Alderson crawled, clambered, crouched, under the ruins for five hours. Air raids were still in spasmodic progress far above him. Someone said: 'Surely no-one can still be alive down there?' But they were.

Alderson dug through to them, to find two persons alive. They were right under a massive commercial refrigerator which threatened to collapse on them as the debris was gradually removed to reach them. Alderson and his team somehow hauled them out from the remains of the cellar. One of these survivors subsequently died, but this did not in any manner detract from the remarkable triple rescue achivements of Thomas Alderson. His was the first GC to be Gazetted.

Harry Errington,
FIREMAN, AUXILIARY FIRE SERVICE

At this stage of the war, the George Cross was being earned, if not yet awarded, almost every day. Only forty-eight hours after the exploits involving Thomas Alderson (or at least, the first of them) it was 17 September and eleven nights into the London Blitz. The capital would be attacked by the Luftwaffe for a further forty-six successive nights, making fifty-seven in all. Some sixty-five years later, it may be hard to visualize the effect of such a sustained onslaught on Londoners, the fabric of the city, and particularly the personnel of the emergency services.

In this instance, just one of hundreds, high explosive and incendiary bombs demolished a building being occupied by the London Auxiliary Fire Service. It had been a three-storey garage before its wartime occupation by the AFS. The floors buckled and broke under the force. About a score of people were killed at once, including some six firemen.

At the time of the main explosion, Harry Errington and two other auxiliary firemen were the only ones in the basement of the building This area had been allocated as a rest room. Not surprisingly, the basement took the weight of the floors collapsing overhead.

The blast blew Errington across the entire basement. He was dazed and injured, but came to sufficiently to be aware of a fire. His first instinct was naturally to hurry towards an exit, but he heard cries for help from his comrades. He at once groped his way towards the voice or voices. He found a man pinned flat on his back by debris. This victim had his legs trapped, so could not move at all. With the fire spreading, the man was in real danger of being burned to death. The heat became so scorching that Errington had to protect himself with a blanket. After working for some minutes with bare, burned, hands, he managed to release the trapped fireman and drag him free from the wreckage and up a narrow stone staircase at the rear. This was made almost impenetrable by being choked with dust and debris. All the time burning matter was continuing to rain into the basement and they were subconsciously aware of a possible further collapse of the whole garage building.

While struggling up to ground level with his charge, Errington saw the second fireman, by then having lost consciousness. So first of all, Errington got the original rescued man into a courtyard and thence through an adjoining building into the relative haven of a London street still under enemy air attack.

Despite the conditions and though being burned and otherwise hurt, Errington returned to find the second fireman. He had been trapped under an outsize radiator, yet Errington forced him free of this and actually carried him up to ground level. Both of Errington's comrades were severely burned and had other injuries, but they survived solely due to him. He had shown not only courage but epic endurance. These qualities epitomized the whole London Fire Service during the Blitz. By the end of 1940, all three firemen had recovered enough to go back on duty. The Blitz was still on . . .

Roy Thomas Harris,
AIR RAID PRECAUTIONS ENGINEERS SERVICE

On the very next day after Errington's rescues, came another GC action associated with air raids. Sometimes the citation gives as good an idea of a deed as a more detailed description. This is roughly what it said about Roy Harris. He was Chief Combustion Officer for Croydon Corporation, and also in the Air Raid Precautions Engineers Service there. Unexploded bombs fell at Langdale Road School, Thornton Heath, near Croydon, on 18 September. Despite being unfamiliar with these weapons, Harris went ahead and dismantled more than one at the school. They were described as very dangerous devices. The postscript to this particular deed was that Roy Harris, then thirty-eight years old, actually joined the Royal Engineers later and reached the rank of lieutenant colonel.

Lieutenant John MacMillan Stevenson Patton,
ROYAL CANADIAN ENGINEERS

Three more days and then a clutch of George Cross actions followed virtually on the same date. During a notorious raid on Vickers aircraft factory at Weybridge in Surrey on 21 September, a big bomb dropped by the Luftwaffe failed to explode – intentionally or otherwise. No Army Bomb Disposal personnel were close at hand yet the location and size of the bomb made it imperative for immediate action.

Although twenty-five-year-old Lieutenant Patton was an officer of the Royal Canadian Engineers, he had no direct experience of bomb disposal. However, he understood the urgency and undertook the task of trying to render it safe. Pondering how best to tackle it, he could not see any apparent way to proceed. Prudently he settled on the next best course; to get it away from its lethal location at Vickers. Patton somehow got the bomb on to a skid without mishap. Then he attached this to a vehicle and started to tow the contraption to a safer spot. When he got to a recently-formed bomb crater a reasonable distance from the factory, the bomb went off unceremoniously and without causing any damage to life or limb or Vickers. One happy ending.

Leonard John Miles,
ARP WARDEN

Late that same evening of 21 September, volunteer ARP warden Leonard Miles was on duty at Ilford in Essex. During a night raid he was warned of imminent danger of an explosion from a nearby bomb. The chances were that it would have had a delayed-action device fitted.

Although Miles was virtually within his own particular shelter at that time, he felt he had to run towards the scene of danger to warn members of the public he knew to be still in their homes. He had actually succeeded in warning some nearby residents before the bomb went off. Miles was then dangerously near to the blast, which inflicted serious injuries on him.

While lying awaiting the ambulance to take him to hospital, he was still conscious and obviously suffering severely. A fellow air raid warden approached him to try to help him, but Miles insisted that the man should attend first to a fire which had been caused by a fractured gas main. Miles symbolized the phrase 'devotion to duty'. He saved several lives by warning people of the impending explosion. His injuries were found to be fatal and he died during that same night of 21–22 September.

Lieutenant Commander Richard John Hammersley Ryan, ROYAL NAVY
Chief Petty Officer Reginald Vincent Ellingworth,
ROYAL NAVY

21 September 1940: still the same day and night.

Lieutenant Commander Ryan and Chief Petty Officer Ellingworth both came from Portsmouth area. They were closely connected with the work of HMS *Vernon* Enemy Mining Section there and both were pre-war members of the Royal Navy. But we must go back to 1939 for the start of this mining story.

Lieutenant Commander John Ouvry, when head of Enemy Mining Section, had gone down into the annals of naval history by being the officer to tackle the first German magnetic mine to be recovered in Britain. These secret weapons had been blocking crucial British sea lanes and sinking ships with alarming frequency until their circuitry could be known and countered. Ouvry rendered safe this first magnetic mine on the mudflats off Shoeburyness, near Southend, when an enemy aircraft had dropped two of them too near the shore. Degaussing counter measures were then implemented to protect ships against them. For this unique heroism, Ouvry was awarded the Distinguished Service Order. If the George Cross had been instituted a year sooner than it was, Ouvry would undoubtedly have won it, for this and other gallantry.

Now it was 1940. A new variation of enemy magnetic mine, designated Type C, was desperately sought by Enemy Mining Section. One came to light in much the same sort of unexpected way as the mines at Shoeburyness. These mines were parachute-laid by aircraft. When an enemy plane crashed at Clacton, Ryan successfully took a mine to pieces to discover its mechanism.

Then later in 1940 magnetic mines started to be used by the Germans both at sea and in a modified form as part of the land Blitz on Britain. Ryan and Ellingworth comprised a typical team of commissioned and non-commissioned officers. As with all the *Vernon* and other personnel who handled enemy mines, these two were always aware of what was at stake.

The principal, if not the sole, hazard of stripping the sort of mines being dropped indiscriminately on London was the arming clock of the fuse. This controlled the likely time of explosion, usually in the region of a mere twenty-two seconds after dropping. Of course, sometimes a mine might fail to go off at the designated delay time which could make it more, or less, dangerous to tackle.

If a mine had not exploded almost on impact with the ground, it might mean that the drop had damaged the arming clock, but not necessarily broken it. In other words, it could start up again at the slightest jolt. So an unexploded mine was far from being safe, but represented still a potentially lethal weapon.

Ryan and Ellingworth made a perfect partnership, with an understanding between them bred of long service in the Royal Navy. They always knew that the maximum time left if a clock should start whirring would be those twenty-two seconds. Probably less. Insufficient to run far enough for safety.

At one stage they overcame half-a-dozen magnetic mines, Ryan playing more than his full part in the procedure. One of these six weapons had fallen into a canal, necessitating Ryan wading into mud up to his midriff. He could scarcely walk, let alone run, if an emergency threatened them. He had to fumble about in the thick, muddy water before he could locate and neutraliaze the fuse. Still assisted by the faithful Ellingworth, Ryan rendered safe another mine at Hornchurch in Essex. It had fallen close to the Royal Air Force airfield at Hornchurch and also a nearby factory making war munitions. This mine was dispatched quickly.

Then they answered a call to an unexploded mine, of the same dangerous type, located at Dagenham. They found this suspended still from its parachute. The setting was a warehouse and the suspension of the mine suggested possible instability of the mechanism.

Lieutenant Commander Ryan and Chief Petty Officer Ellingworth were both killed instantly when it blew up . . .

Ryan is commemorated in the Haslar Royal Naval Cemetery at Gosport. Haslar faces the historic narrow entrance to Portsmouth Harbour and can be seen from the shore base of HMS *Vernon* across the water. Chief Petty Officer Ellingworth is commemorated at Milton Cemetery in Portsmouth. This is close to Fratton Park, where practically every member of the Royal Navy has seen Portsmouth FC play at some time or another. So it is safe to say that the chief petty officer had also watched from one of the four sides: the south stand, north stand, Fratton end or Eastney end.

Norman Tunna,
GREAT WESTERN RAILWAY SHUNTER

The initial big Blitz on Merseyside burst forth on 26 September 1940. Enemy action over the Liverpool port area resulted in a scattering of serious fires involving railway and dock warehouse properties. In the Morpeth dock region of Birkenhead, the familiar network of railway lines was crammed with trains. Some of the goods trains were being discharged and reloaded; others already had armaments of every shape and scale. Next day these were due to go aboard ships or barges.

During the raid, a large number of incendiary bombs spattered on and about the goods station and sidings. Norman Tunna was a shunter. He was aware that among the wagons in the goods yard stood a train with half-a-dozen of its wagons full of highly explosive ammunition; 500-pound bombs, petrol in cans and fuses. A potentially lethal cocktail.

Most of the incendiaries were extinguished by prompt action of the staff on duty, thus avoiding the danger of damage. However, a serious fire did develop from other incendiaries falling in one section of the station premises.

As all this was in progress, and the raid on Merseyside still proceeding loudly, Tunna considered it his duty to walk the length of the armament train. He suddenly saw signs of burning material falling from one of the high-explosive wagons. He discovered two incendiary bombs blazing in the sheeted open wagon and knew that this particular one was carrying 250-pound bombs.

Tunna raced back to the engine of the train, drew a bucket of water, jogged back to the burning rail wagon and threw the bucketful on the flames. This seemed to extinguish the fire from the actual incendiary, which must have been on the track under the wagon.

Tunna felt that the fire had probably spread inside the wagon itself. Removing the sheeting, he climbed on to the wagon to see another incendiary wedged between two of the high-explosive bombs. The top layer of the bombs was hot; alarmingly so. He managed to manipulate his shunting pole to force a space between the bombs, allowing the incendiary to fall on to the railway line.

However . . . the wagon's woodwork was ablaze and the bombs were perilously close. Tunna's presence of mind continued. Armed with the fairly primitive stirrup pump issued for such a purpose, he succeeded in spraying water on the bombs until he felt sure in his mind that the fire was out. As an extra precaution, Tunna told the train driver to take the whole train under the nearby water column and drench it. Norman Tunna's decisive countermeasures eliminated the risk of serious explosions from the heavily-laden armament train. If it had once caught fire and exploded, the severity of the results 'would have been difficult to measure'. So said the citation to his George Cross.

Wing Commander Laurence Frank Sinclair,
ROYAL AIR FORCE

After dark on 30 September 1940, a bomber was about to take off from RAF Wattisham in Suffolk. Although the defensive Battle of Britain was still officially not yet over, the Royal Air Force had started engaging in offensive operations. Tragically, as the bomber took off, it burst into flames.

The flat Suffolk landscape was suddenly thrown into relief. Wing Commander Sinclair ran towards the scene with others to try to help, but two 250-pound bombs exploded before anyone could reach the plane. Sinclair ran on undeterred, knowing that two more bombs lurked in the aircraft, waiting to go off. Using a combination of courage and initiative, he dashed into the fire and summoning all his strength, dragged the air gunner to a safe distance. Sinclair showed utter disregard for his own safety in trying to save one of the aircrew.

In emergencies such as this, no-one could ever know the outcome until it was all over. Whatever happened, nothing could detract from the Wing Commander's action. He could so easily have suffered fatally from it. In fact, Sinclair survived, but the air gunner had sustained such severe injuries that he died from them later. Sir Laurence Sinclair later reached the rank of Air Vice Marshal.

Sub Lieutenant William Horace Taylor,
ROYAL NAVAL VOLUNTEER RESERVE

The date of this next deed was 7 October 1940. The citation for Sub Lieutenant Taylor must rank among the shortest ever announced for such an award. It was made 'for great gallantry and undaunted devotion to duty in connection with mine disposal in late September/early October 1940, and in particular with an extremely dangerous operation at the Royal Air Force Depot, Uxbridge'. Taylor became a Lieutenant Commander RNVR and survived the war. He held appointments in the Scout Association for twenty-eight years.

George Walter Inwood,
SECTION COMMANDER, HOME GUARD

Prior to their infamous Blitz on Coventry, the Germans made an equally damaging air onslaught on the larger neighbouring urban complex of Birmingham. The great Midlands manufacturing city sustained this sudden shock over the night of 15–16 October 1940. It was against the background of the after effects of the raid that the next George Cross was earned.

George Inwood was a section commander with a battalion of the local Home Guard, and in this capacity he led his men to assist in any way they could. Inwood was told that one explosion had resulted in an unknown number of persons being trapped below ground level in a particular house. That would have been bad enough, but gas had penetrated throughout this cellar area, so that none of the people down there remained conscious.

Some of Inwood's section helped lower him into the remains of the cellar by means of a rope. With difficulty and summoning maximum effort, Inwood extricated two males from their underground cell. Having saved the lives of these two men, he refused to give up. Inwood had inhaled quantities of the escaping gas himself, but was lowered down a second time to try to save others. The fumes, however, had penetrated his lungs more than he could have realized and he collapsed during the strain of attempting the

21

repeat rescue. He had done his duty, but could not survive the lethal nature of the gas and died.

Second Lieutenant Alexander Fraser Campbell,
ROYAL ENGINEERS
Sergeant Michael Gibson,
ROYAL ENGINEERS

Two fateful days of the Blitz on Coventry were 17 and 18 October 1940. On the first of these dates, the Luftwaffe struck two of several famous factories carrying out war work – both part of the Triumph Engineering works. The raid had the dual effect of damaging both factories and stopping vital production. Added to this, an unexploded bomb forced the evacuation of residents whose homes lay close to the works.

Second Lieutenant Campbell was the Royal Engineers officer called to deal with this bomb, but at once he detected the presence of a delayed-action fuse. With no chance of extracting this fuse without endangering personnel, property, and himself, he decided prudently to have it taken by lorry to a remote location.

The team mounted the bomb on the lorry with meticulous caution and then Campbell crouched down beside it while they were en route to their destination. In this way, he hoped to hear if the clock to the fuse should start; if it did, and he heard it above the sound of the vehicle, they could halt and shelter. This did not prove necessary, and the bomb was disposed of without further incident. Sergeant Michael Gibson was with Campbell during the officer's work in Coventry.

On the following day, they were summoned to a second un-exploded bomb in Coventry. The two of them started on their procedure of trying to defuse the bomb where it lay. Tragically, there came the too frequent conclusion to their efforts. The bomb fired, killing both men.

Sub Lieutenant Jack Maynard Cholmondeley Easton,
ROYAL NAVAL VOLUNTEER RESERVE
Able Seaman Bennett Southwell, ROYAL NAVY

On the self same day that Army personnel were tackling bombs in Coventry, Naval men were being rushed to unexploded mines in London and, as in the Coventry case, two servicemen were involved. The outcome was similar in one respect, although different in another . . .

Although as in all such cases the officer bore the ultimate responsibility, a non-commissioned serviceman ran risks equally as extreme. So the date was still 17 October 1940. As usual, London's heavily peopled East End had been hit both by bombs and landmines. Sub Lieutenant Easton and Able Seaman Southwell responded to the report of a huge unexploded mine in Hoxton.

Because of the size of the mine, and the havoc it could cause, it seemed as if half of Hoxton had been evacuated from their terraced homes. Easton and Southwell picked their way through the eerily empty roads to the one where the mine had been found. Not that it had needed much finding. The massive weapon had destroyed the roof of the house in its descent, and now hung through an aperture it had forced in the ceiling. The nose of the mine was mere inches above the flooring.

Easton assessed the precarious situation and settled for trying to tackle the rendering safe process there and then. It would have been too risky to attempt removal of the mine. But then again, it was also risky to attack it where it was. He made the only decision possible when faced with such a dilemma. He told Southwell: 'stay in the passage and just give me the tools as I need them.'

A minute or so later, the hanging mine slipped slightly. Bricks fell. The chimney-pot collapsed. Easton heard clockwork whirring. They had ten to twenty seconds to get out. 'Run for it,' he called to Southwell.

The able seaman scampered out into the road. Easton ran, too, and just managed to hurl himself into a surface air raid shelter. The mine went off with almost unimaginable force. Easton was knocked unconscious. When he came to, he had been buried by surrounding masonry from the shelter and elsewhere. Rescuers got to him and dug him from the rubble.

Meanwhile, Southwell seemed to have escaped the explosion, but the blast caught up with him and killed him. The effect of the mine was so intense that it wiped out half-a-dozen Hoxton streets and it was, in fact, six weeks before the body of Southwell came to light among the debris of that day. Easton did survive, but with a broken back. He had to remain in plaster for a whole year. Later he resumed more normal Naval service when as a lieutenant he took charge of a minesweeper.

A change now from landmines to seamines. The war went on.

Sub Lieutenant John Herbert Babington,
ROYAL NAVAL VOLUNTEER RESERVE

Normally, Naval officers dealt with mines and Army personnel with bombs and occasionally, RAF officers could be responsible. But sometimes, as in this case, the demarcation line became blurred between Army and Navy.

Sub Lieutenant Babington had been associated with magnetic mines during the first twelve months of the war, as well as various kinds of enemy bombs. This incident involved a bomb dropped on the Naval dockyard of Chatham. The Kent base was, with Portsmouth and Devonport, one of the three premier Naval centres in Britain. An earlier bomb, similar in appearance to this one, had cost an RAF ofiicer his life, possibly through the presence of newly-introduced devices to prevent stripping in the case of delayed-action or failure to fire.

Babington offered to tackle this present bomb, which had lodged itself in a hole some sixteen feet deep. These were still comparatively early days in discovering the circuits of both bombs and mines.

Men lowered Babington into the pit so that he could fix a line to the fuse of the bomb. The line snapped and he had no choice but to be lowered to ground level and prepare for a second attempt. This proved just as difficult and Babington then had to repeat the procedure. Third time lucky could have been a phrase invented for the Sub Lieutenant. This time he did manage to loop the line successfully and withdraw the fuse. After that it was fairly easy, if raising a bomb out of a sixteen-foot hole could ever be called easy. Babington reverted to sea mines after this and survived the war. He was later headmaster, successively, of Diss Grammar School and the Royal Hospital School in Suffolk.

Lieutenant Robert Selby Armitage,
ROYAL NAVAL VOLUNTEER RESERVE

To appreciate the achievements of the HMS Enemy Mining Section, it must be remembered that each officer was aware of the tragedies that had already befallen colleagues. So to set the scene for the list of Lieutenant Armitage's successes, the following took place in August 1940.

A mine had been returned to HMS *Vernon* for stripping to discover its contents. But the Germans knew that they must do all they could to prevent their circuits and secrets being uncovered. In the mining shed, the last nut was being loosened from the rear door of the enemy mine. Then Petty Officer Fletcher held the door in his hands. The suction of the rubber jointing band between it and the main body yielded a bit. Then a sudden whirring sound. A flash. A roar.

The explosion blew the roof off the mining shed. Blackened men, brutally burned, were helped out by the south door. The shed was a shambles. The sky gaped through the roof. There was glass and blood everywhere. A contorted figure lay flung into a corner; a sailor collected charred remains; Mr Cook, a commissioned gunner, was dying. Little was left of Petty Officer Fletcher. Bits of tangled metal lay all around. Miraculously, the lieutenant standing behind Fletcher did not die. But six lives were lost.

From then on, all mines recovered were taken to a remote spot in the South Downs. The scientists reassembled the remains of the mine and were able, in time, to design equipment to counter the enemy's 'prevention-of-stripping' scheme.

So intent were the Germans on preventing the Royal Navy from stripping recovered mines, that they actually dropped pseudo mines from the air designed solely to kill personnel and thus discourage them from future attempts. They dropped one inland without the crucial components a real mine would have had. The device was dropped, planted, with the explicit intention of killing personnel handling it. The weapon had a triple booby trap . . .

Armitage was prominent in dealing with this fresh hazard, but at the same time he handled many cases of unexploded or delayed-action mines in the south-east of England. It was still the historic period of September and October 1940. The Battle of Britain was finally declared won on 31 October.

It would be repetitious to recite too many incidents conquered by Armitage. His officer colleague described one of these in this way: 'We were working near a building on a Type D, and the clockwork fuse started to go. The gardens were damned difficult to negotiate. I hopped over a fence or two. Armitage was behind me. When I reckoned I'd got far enough, I got my head down quick. None too soon really, for the thing blew up a couple of seconds later. When it was all over, I got up and looked for Armitage. I couldn't see him anywhere. Then from the far corner of the garden something stirred. Armitage got up from a compost heap and walked towards me. Actually, it was pretty bad. He was only thirty yards off when it fired – too close for comfort.'

Next day, Armitage was working as usual. None of them wanted just to sit still and think for too long. One of Armitage's mines was actually found hanging from a tree in Orpington, Kent. The lieutenant had to climb a ladder to get to it. If the clock had started to tick on that occasion, he would not have had time to escape.

Lieutenant Commander Armitage lived out his life at his Oxfordshire home in Nettlebed.

Acting Flight Lieutenant Wilson Hodgson Charlton

Over the two momentous months of September and October 1940, Flight Lieutenant Charlton had dealt with the astounding total of 200 unexploded bombs. He was responsible for rendering safe bombs in an area comprising the greater part of two counties. Over this period the potentially lethal double century of weaponry was tackled both by day and night. In rather prosaically and understated tone, the official announcement of his award ends, Charlton 'successfully undertook many dangerous missions with undaunted and unfailing courage'. It seems scarcely credible that not a single accident occurred during so massive an achievement – testimony to Charlton's courage and also his skill. He was in a Japanese PoW camp for the final three years of the conflict and, after that, returned to bomb disposal.

Major Herbert John Leslie Barefoot

Although fifty-three years old when the Blitz began – and having served in the First World War – Major Barefoot was one of the first Royal Engineers to disarm unexploded bombs during the autumn of 1940. His particular claim to fame in this sphere was that he had to face the first suspended parachute magnetic mine. In recognizing his operations in Bomb Disposal, the authorities especially referred to the inspiration he gave to others of the Corps of Royal Engineers assisting him.

Sergeant Raymond Mayhew Lewin

The date: 3 November 1940. The place: Malta. The subject of the action: Sergeant Lewin. He was the captain of an aircraft on a night bombing mission from the already-beleaguered island outpost of Malta. Hardly had the bomber taken off when it began to lose what little height it had gained. It sank towards the Maltese uplands behind Luqa. A few seconds later it crashed into a hillside. Fire spread searingly.

Lewin extricated himself and saw three of his crew of four climbing safely out of the escape hatch. After ordering them to run clear of the flames, he ran around a burning wing containing full fuel tanks already ablaze. He crawled under the wing to rescue his injured second pilot. Lewin himself had sustained a cracked kneecap and severe contusions on his face and legs, yet he half dragged, half carried the second pilot some forty yards from the aircraft to a dip in the ground. Lewin lay on him just as the bombs aboard the aircraft exploded.

He performed this rescue in the dark of the hillside and knowing for sure that the bombs and petrol tanks must explode. The only uncertain thing was precisely when they would. Sergeant Lewin died just over a year later as a pilot officer.

Special Constable Brandon Moss

Coventry on the night of 14 November 1940. The first raiders crossed the coast over Lyme Bay, Dorset, at 6.17 p.m. They arrived over Coventry at 8.15 p.m. to drop incendiaries as markers; then 437 aircraft converged from different directions and dropped 394 tons of high explosives and 127 parachute mines.

In this raid of infamy, a quarter of a million people suffered for eleven hours under a full moon. Their little huddled houses, many factories, and the historic medieval cathedral were all hit. Most of the fires were around the cathedral area. The cathedral itself was destroyed, but became a symbol of strength. and defiance for the country. Standards, Alvis, Daimler and other works were damaged: twenty-one in all. Two hundred gas mains were fractured, the Army handled many unexploded bombs and 0bserver Corps plotters tracked the enemy despite twenty near-misses on their headquarters. Three hundred and eighty civilians were killed on that night . . .

If the cathedral symbolized the spirit of Britain after that night, symbolizing the spirit of Coventry was Brandon Moss.

As the Luftwaffe unleashed their loads on Coventry Cathedral and the city centre generally, Special Constable Moss stood on duty watching it all come down around him; roll after roll of bomb blasts in his ears. Then suddenly the screech of another high explosive. The bomb hit a house, flattening it like an open hand on a house of cards.

Under the wreckage, the three occupants lay buried. Three citizens of Coventry. Moss led a rescue party in literally clawing, clearing, an entry towards the trapped victims. The rescuers found their going progressively more dangerous, due to collapsing debris and leaking gas.

'They'll never get through,' a spectator was heard to say.

When conditions finally became really risky, Moss went on, and in, alone. He burrowed a clearance, animal-like, and tunnelled through this limited space to the trapped people. One by one he saved them unaided; dragging them out towards the surface and the air. Then the others in the rescue team took over and helped him.

By that time it was around midnight and bombs were still falling fast and regularly. Moss had hardly emerged with the last survivor than he heard someone say:

'Some more buried next door.'

'Come on then,' he called to the rescuers.

Hour upon hour they toiled on amid the raid and the wreckage. After several hours, the workers had to stop from exhaustion. Moss himself went on, Beams were creaking and falling, while crumbling and collapsing walls threw up a fog of dust. Still Moss struggled on. 'We've got to get them,' he insisted.

By his supreme, almost superhuman, efforts, he was responsible for recovering four bodies plus one person actually alive. So this second rescue had been worthwhile. He had toiled for over seven hours, from 11 p.m. until 6.30 a.m. Only at dawn did he agree to pause.

He had gone on, too, knowing that there was a delayed-action bomb in the doorway of a public house a mere twenty yards down the same road – barely the length of a cricket pitch away. The rescued survivors lived – and so did Coventry. Hardly anyone quit the city. But the raid had cost those precious 380 lives.

Lieutenant William Marsdel Eastman,
ROYAL ARMY ORDNANCE CORPS
Captain Robert Llewellyn Jephson-Jones,
ROYAL ARMY ORDNANCE CORPS

These two officers were gazetted for the George Cross on Christmas Eve 1940. The setting for their deeds was Malta. Jephson-Jones was actually residing in Malta when war was declared, while Eastman went there in March 1940 with the RAOC. The siege of Malta started in June, when it became the focus for fierce air raids by both the Italian and German air forces. This was the period when the aerial defence of the island depended on three biplanes, affectionately nicknamed Faith, Hope and Charity. The rest of that story continues in the chapter on Malta GC.

Meanwhile, the bombs started to cascade down on the crucial defences of the island and also on the ancient stonework of its capital. At this early stage of the war, the Army had not yet organized the Royal Engineers Bomb Disposal for overseas duty, so the plethora of unexploded mines and bombs had to be dealt with usually by the Royal Army Ordnance Corps. The Royal Navy handled any dropped within the Malta dockyard region, while the Royal Air Force took reaponsibility for those in their own airfield areas.

But this left the majority of the weapons to the RAOC, which really meant Jephson-Jones and Eastman. From the very beginning of the aerial onslaught, these two officers shared the daily hazards involved. For five months they were solely in charge. And in this spell, they neutralized no fewer than 275 bombs between them. This represented an average of virtually one bomb a day each.

The remarkable outcome was that they both managed to survive such odds and live through the rest of the war. By the end of November 1940, they received a hundred-times-earned respite when Royal Engineers Bomb Disposal assumed their duties. Both Jephson-Jones and Eastman rose to the rank of brigadier later in their distinguished Army careers.

Lieutenant Harold Reginald Newgass,
ROYAL NAVAL VOLUNTEER RESERVE

The landmine menace spread north to Coventry, Glasgow and Liverpool. On 28 November 1940, one fell and failed to explode on a gasometer of the Garston Gas Works on Merseyside. The dense assembly of factories around the area came to a total halt.

The mine had penetrated the top of the gasholder, with its parachute actually enmeshed in the hole it had caused to the roof. This ripped roof meant that gas was escaping. It also caused the dangling mine to repose on the floor of the gasometer. The mine looked ominous, with its dark nose in a fathom or more of stagnant water lapping the floor of the structure.

When Newgass arrived on this scene, the mine was resting up against a six-foot-high pillar supporting still more iron pillars and the gasometer roof. It was all appearing very shaky. The fuse in the mine, needless to say, faced the brick pillar so Newgass could not tackle it at once. With the mine in this precarious position, and actually inside an active gasometer, it somehow had to be turned.

It was later considered that this situation must have been among the most dangerous ever faced by a Naval officer confronting an enemy mine, whether on land or by the coast. Newgass went ahead quite alone. Due to the escaping gas and generally foetid and foul air, he had to breathe with the aid of oxygen from one of six cylinders he used altogether.

The whole operation could be measured by these cylinders and how much he could achieve before he had to renew one. Newgass did his reconnaissance while breathing from cylinder number one. During the next one, he had to carry a ladder and his technical tools for the task. A change of cylinder and then he sandbagged the mine's nose, clambered on to the brick pillar and secured the mine to the roof.

Yet another change of cylinder to number four, and still unaided Newgass turned the mine and went through the dangerous drill of handling fuse, primer and detonator. The penultimate cylinder enabled him to breathe long enough to loosen the timing clock; always an apprehensive moment. Finally,

31

he slid the clock free from the other mechanism in the mine and the whole evil weapon was rendered harmless. Newgass could hardly have been sorry to climb out of that gasometer. He had avoided potential loss of life and property – and he lived to the age of eighty-eight.

Sub Lieutenant Peter Victor Danckwerts,
ROYAL NAVAL VOLUNTEER RESERVE

Landmines on London. Because they were mines instead of bombs, HMS *Vernon* Enemy Mining Section was called on to deal with them. For whatever reason the mines had not exploded, they represented immediate danger to the population of the capital, already suffering severely from the Blitz. The mines might have failed to go off due to mechanical failure, or they might have incorporated a delay device to cause added terror, discomfort or death. Whatever the reason, they had to be made safe somehow. And when they were, *Vernon*'s officers were being cheered by Londoners whose homes had been saved from destruction.

Two officers paired off to head for a reported mine at Woolwich. Here, however, they found that it had already been successfully dealt with by a certain Sub Lieutenant Danckwerts. Two other officers joined them, breaking the news that they, too, had been beaten to their particular mine by Danckwerts.

So who was this comparative novice? Peter Danckwerts had been born in Portsmouth, so was especially suited to service with HMS *Vernon*. Late in 1940, at the times of these 'escapades' in London, he had been a bare one-and-a-half months in the Royal Naval Volunteer Reserve. He had started to tackle the mines with no definite orders to do so, and without the full gear for the job.

Danckwerts received training, of course, but at that stage in the Blitz, he had never even seen a live mine, much less actually touched one or tried to make it safe. Despite lacking these basic advantages, he started work on his series of mines for two days and two nights, virtually with no break. The total number he neutralized in that period reached the staggering total of sixteen.

One particular case has been quoted as typical 'Danckwerts'. In the company of a Royal Navy chief petty officer, he was directed to not one mine but two. The sight confronting them would have frightened most onlookers. In a warehouse, the weapons hung by their caught-up parachutes. Their twin noses, containing the firing mechanisms, sniffed the floor. The Sub Lieutenant and Chief Petty Officer advanced quietly. But the vibration of their tread caused the clock in one of the pair to start. This could only mean one thing; the mine could still be live and likely to actuate at any time.

Danckwerts and the chief retreated without ceremony.

The clock stopped ticking.

They returned to the mines. They heard no further sound, so proceeded with their routine. Although the clock had stopped, they both knew that any timepiece was susceptible to the slightest shock and if restarted it could fire the mine within seconds. Danckwerts kept his nerve and his hands steady. He extracted the crucial firing fuse, then did the same to the second mine and felt a little easier.

He went on to survive the war and enjoyed a distinguished career in Cambridge.

Sub Lieutenant John Bryan Peter Duppa-Miller,
ROYAL NAVAL VOLUNTEER RESERVE
Able Seaman Stephen John Tuckwell,
ROYAL NAVY

It could be imagined that in theory all cases of mine or bomb disposal might be similar. In practice, though, infinite variations existed dependent on where the weapon happened to have fallen, what condition it was in when found, how it had to be tackled, what sort of circuitry was inside it, whether it was likely to go off and lastly, whether it killed or injured anyone.

Sub Lieutenant Duppa-Miller and Able Seaman Tuckwell were a team. They had chalked up a number of successes since early in the Blitz. Any one of these jobs could have earned them a medal. The incident selected for official recognition happened when an enemy mine came to earth, or water, on the mud of a river running into Barking Creek, Essex.

The circumstances that distinguished this job were that Duppa-Miller first of all had to get hold of a canoe, mount it with their kit on a River Fire Serviee fire float and set off in search of the reported position of the mine. At a certain stage up the creek, they transferred from the fire float into the canoe. After a bit of paddling, the black outline of the mine hove into view, its nose embedded in the mad.

The two men were on the kind of terms that could only be developed from having shared past dangers. Duppa-Miller offered Tuckwell the chance to leave him to deal with the mine alone. But the rating said that the officer would have to handle his duty with hands under water so would require the sailor to give him the tools.

The drill started. Duppa-Miller extracted one of the two fuses, but the other one remained beyond his grasp. Something had to be done. The location was not an isolated one, and some drivers of cranes were watching their activities from a nearby wharf. Duppa-Miller needed their assistance, so went over to explain his plan. Then he and Tuckwell returned to the mud of the creek. They slung ropes carefully around the slimy, slippery mine casing, and then the drivers of the cranes started to help ease the live mine from the water. It squelched across the mud and finally they raised it to wharf level. The drill still had to be gone through, before that second fuse could be detached from the circuitry. But at least Duppa-Miller and Tuckwell were on the wharf and no longer floundering about in a foot or more of murky water. Until the mine had been raised free of the mud, the Naval disposal team had been working blind. Not the best way to have to gamble on your life. Duppa-Miller held education appointments in Africa from 1945 to 1957.

Sub Lieutenant Richard Valentine Moore,
ROYAL NAVAL VOLUNTEER RESERVE

Twenty-four-year-old Sub Lieutenant Moore was awarded the George Cross 'for gallantry and undaunted devotion to duty in connection with bomb disposal'. Although he had no practical training, he was called upon in an emergency and disarmed five mines.

Moore reached the rank of lieutenant commander, RNVR, and after the war went on to a notable career in atomic energy at Harwell, Risley and Calder Hall. He became a Director of Reactor Design followed by a Faraday Lecturer.

William Mosedale,
STATION OFFICER AND RESCUE OFFICER, BIRMINGHAM FIRE BRIGADE

About a fortnight before Christmas 1940, on the night of 12 December, an auxiliary fire station in Birmingham was completely demolished by a very large bomb. A number of auxiliary firemen were trapped in the station, while civilians had been buried in an adjoining house which was also demolishied.

Forty-five-year-old Station Officer Mosedale immediately began tunnelling and propping operations, with the aim of getting through to the control room. Hundreds of tons of debris shrouded the site, and Mosedale knew that at any moment he might be buried by a further collapse.

When the first tunnel was completed and the control room reached, he found that some men still could not be extricated. He carried out another similar operation from a different direction again getting through successfully to the control room. Five men were found, one dead and the others injured. Mosedale crawled through the aperture and administered oxygen to the injured, who were removed to safety through the tunnel. Without this escape route, they must have perished.

The entrance to the cellar of the adjacent private house was barred by brick debris. Mosedale next directed operations for removing this wreckage, only to find that the cellar itself had caved in. But he persevered, as he knew there were people down there. After a time, the rescuers managed to hack through to the cellar area, to find seven people trapped. Three had been killed outright by the collapsing structure. Mosedale gave oxygen to the other four and extricated them, with the help of his team.

Back in the fire station again, or what remained of it, he

35

commenced more tunnelling to reach other men known to be trapped below. They were thought to number four or more. The situation was the same as faced when Mosedale tunnelled towards the control room. Nevertheless, he dug through to the cellar to find four men alive. The same urgent drill was applied; oxygen, help in squeezing through the debris, eventual lifting to stretchers and safety.

Soon after the last man had been evacuated, the cellar gave way completely, so it had been a race against time, as Mosedale realized all the while. He carried out all the rescues under intense air bombardment on Birmingham and his efforts extended over a superhuman twelve hours. Mosedale was certainly directly responsible for saving the lives of twelve men. The official recognition referred to resource beyond his obvious quality of gallantry. By this stage of the Blitz, it had become patently apparent that the war would involve civilians as much as service personnel.

Acting Captain Michael Floud Blaney,
CORPS OF ROYAL ENGINEERS

Three dates in 1940 were cited in the award to Acting Captain Blaney; 18 September, 20 October and 13 December. Three days spread over three months. An unexploded bomb was reported in London early on 18 September. It fell in the middle of Manor Way, near a major road junction. Its location caused disruption to traffic to the London Docks, Royal Arsenal, and other centres crucial to war work. Blaney removed the bomb, so that minimum disturbance occurred and war workers could complete their various journeys.

On the second date of 20 October, another unexploded bomb fell in the same general district – Park Avenue, East Ham, in the East End of London. Despite a pair of deadly time fuses fitted to this bomb, Blaney neutralized it, working alone as he insisted on doing in instances like this. Once again, public services and war traffic were spared disturbance and Blaney survived for a second time.

The bomb on 13 December really represented a continuation of the case of Lieutenant Archer and his men at Swansea. As 1940 neared its end, German bombs became more advanced, with combinations of fuses to be tackled by Bomb Disposal. This third unexploded bomb, now designated UXB for short, had fallen on Romford Road, Manor Park, London. It was uncovered about twelve feet below ground level. This was fitted with a Type-17 delayed-action clockwork fuse coupled with a Type-50, whose express purpose was to delay the explosion until the bomb was moved or tapped.

Captain Blaney had Lieutenant James with him and they reached Romford Road soon after the bomb was exposed. They phoned for steam sterilizing equipment, one of the techniques introduced since the start of hostilities. However, this did not arrive, due to the breakdown of a truck transporting it.

But they did have at their disposal two of the then-latest devices for dealing with clockwork fuses; an experimental version of a new magnetic clock stopper and an electric stethoscope. This early clock stopper or Q-coil was designed to stop movement of the clock inside the fuse by magnetizing it strongly. The stethoscope was an electric sound amplifier fitted with headphones, so that an operator could listen to any ticking within a bomb, either while beside it or some way off. Both these were still at a comparatively primitive stage of their evolution, but both were quite advanced conceptions for 1940.

Captain Blaney decided that the Q-coil should be applied to the bomb, which should then be very carefully hoisted out of its nest and taken to a nearby open space, where it could be dealt with conveniently. He based his calculation on the then-current notion that after three or four days the Type-50 fuse was inert.

When the hoisting sling was passed round the bomb, they found that the Q-coil was in the way of the lifting tackle. Blaney took the only possible course open to him at that moment. He ordered that the bomb should be lifted without the Q-coil, which should be immediately refitted when the bomb had been brought to the surface. A block and tackle was fastened to a joist of the adjacent house and connected to the sling round the bomb. Everybody available hauled at the rope until the bomb emerged and hung a couple of feet above the mouth of the hole. It was swinging a little freely, so Blaney stepped up to stop the motion.

That was the moment when the bomb exploded.

Hanging above the ground, the bomb was in as bad a position as possible. Both officers, a staff sergeant, a lance corporal, five Sappers, and a superintendent of police watching, were all killed. Ten men.

The non-commissioned officer, Staff Sergeant Fox, who was listening to the electrical stethoscope from behind cover had an escape typical of the chances in this kind of work. A few seconds before the explosion, Staff Sergeant Roberts, who was killed, had asked Fox to take his place at the headphones because, while sitting there listening, he had become cramped and cold. The stethoscope was attached while the bomb was being hauled from the pit, but no ticking had been heard at any stage.

The Type-50 fuse was assumed to have caused the detonation. Some two or three weeks before this disaster, the No. 1 fuse-extractor, or 'Freddy' as it was called, began to be distributed to Bomb Disposal personnel. This ultimately deprived the Type-50 fuse of much of its lethal sting.

Sub Lieutenant Geoffrey Gledhill Turner

Sub Lieutenant Turner rendered many mines safe in the autumn of 1940. A typical example of his early batch of unexploded mines was the metallic monster that parachuted squarely on to the London Midland and Scottish station at Sheffield. Turner had to handle not only the mine but the parachute too.

One of the mines that were dropped over Liverpool on 21 December 1940 also had its parachute still attached. Landing on a wool factory, the chute had been partially caught up, so that the nose of the mine nuzzled against the floor. More awkward still than this, the main fuse happened to be concealed. The weapon weighed something approaching a ton and so altogether Turner was faced with a delicate job to extract the fuse, like a dentist taking out a tooth without being able to see the patient's mouth. He managed it as usual.

The location of another mine facing him was Seaforth, Lancashire. It had burrowed itself in the back yard of a modest house there, quite near to the Southport to Liverpool railway track. Turner improvised with a wire to get the mine shifted into a better position for him to get at the fuse. He hit a snag. When he tried to withdraw the fuse, he realized that it had been broken by the impact of dropping. He had half of it, but the crucial clock and firing apparatus remained behind.

He knew this was a dangerous moment even by his standards, so attempted to get out the rest of the fuse with his bare hands or fingers. But just when it seemed to be almost achieved, he heard the familiar ominous whirr of the clock. Turner got as far away as he could, as quickly as he could. No burst followed the sound of the clockwork, so after a while he went back – always a hard choice.

At his first tentative touch on the fuse, the clockwork commenced once more. Turner did not know how long, or short, a time it would run before activating the fuse. He turned round and ran again, but the mine went off. Only yards away, he felt the shock-waves. He was wounded, yes, but somehow the mine did not kill him.

Turner won the George Medal in addition to the George Cross, and later in the war transferred to the Marine Commandos for a bit of peace and quiet! He took part in the D-Day invasion and became a Commander, Royal Naval Volunteer Reserve.

Sub Lieutenant Francis Haffey Brooke-Smith,
ROYAL NAVAL RESERVE

During the latter days of 1940, an air raid on the general Manchester/Mersey area left an unexploded mine on a Fire Service fire float in the Manchester Ship Canal. The weapon had lodged itself within the deck locker, which ran beside the vessel's engine room. It was stuck obstinately in this situation and looked as if it would be resistant to rendering safe where it lay.

Sub Lieutenant Brooke-Smith employed the aid of a rope to help him haul the mine a little out of its lodgement. His next job involved positioning his whole body on the engine casing. This was far from level and worse than that, Brooke-Smith was forced to start his routine while working with his head downwards. At this precarious angle, he somehow plugged the fuse with a safety gag. Then the thing he most dreaded happened. The fuse clock started its sickening whirring sound. Brooke-Smith did not panic; he lay where he was and tried to stop the clock before it set off the fuse and the mine.

The Sub Lieutenant was working in excruciating conditions, having to experiment with the safety gag entirely without visual contact with the fuse. He went ahead gingerly by the experience of touch, as a blind man might do. In this inauspicious setting, he must have thought that he might not get away with it. The safety gag was also a relatively recent development in dismantling techniques at that date, and Brooke-Smith had never tried it before that day. He got the gag in place and stopped the clockwork in time.

Sub Lieutenant Brooke-Smith survived the war but died at the very young age of only thirty-four.

Chapter Two

1941

Acting Corporal James Patrick Scully,
ROYAL PIONEER CORPS

After the plethora of George Cross awards in 1940, the first deed to be recognized with the honour in 1941 was not until 8 March.

The Blitz on Merseyside caused one group of houses to be utterly demolished. Corporal Scully formed part of a rescue team sent to search for any trapped survivors.

Scully did, in fact, hear the voices of a man and a woman. With the greatest difficulty he managed to penetrate the familiar debris in the aftermath of an air raid. He reached the point where they had been buried, while the officer directing operations, Lieutenant Chittenden, followed him closely. They had wood as props to help shore up the surrounding area, but there was no means of cutting it into convenient lengths for the purpose

A rescue party then arrived with tools to cut the wood into more suitable shoring sizes. All the men worked hard to clear away the wreckage, knowing the serious situation of the survivors. Scully remained with these two trapped people and prevented any more debris falling on them.

The team managed to insert a long plank to take most of the weight of the rubble, but some further falls resulted in the props beginning to sway out of position perilously. There was then a very real danger of the entire mass crumbling and burying the man and woman permanently.

Scully knew that this could happen, so placed his back squarely under the plank to try to support the props and prevent them giving way completely. He succeeded in steadying them for a time, but gradually the weight increased to an intolerable amount, until the props started to slip. This left Scully holding one end of the plank and Lieutenant Chittenden supporting the other. Both men were risking everything now.

At this stage, Scully could have got away, but he knew that if he did so the debris would fall further and probably kill the survivors. He stayed under the plank. Gradually the weight forced him down until he lay right across the trapped man.

Chittenden continued to hold one end of the plank. He reached over and supported Scully's head to prevent it being pressed into the jumble of debris. Chittenden managed to keep Scully's face just clear, but the officer, too, was becoming exhausted. Despite this nightmare condition, both men kept up their spirits and continued to talk to the woman survivor. The man by then was unconscious nearly all the time.

Scully remained in this position throughout the night until other rescuers were able to reach him and the two casualties. Fully seven hours had elapsed since the start of the incident. The corporal knew from the outset that there would be a grave risk of injury or even death, as adjacent high walls appeared about to collapse. Had this happened, they would all have been buried under tons of masonry. Scully risked his life to save the two people and although the position frequently looked hopeless, Lieutenant Chittenden stayed with him. The officer was awarded the George Medal, while Scully earned the George Cross.

Lieutenant Ernest Oliver Gidden,
ROYAL NAVAL VOLUNTEER RESERVE

It will always be remembered as the Charing Cross mine. On 17 April 1941, the air attacks were almost over for a time. Hitler was about to turn his attention and troops towards Russia. Lieutenant Gidden reported for duty at the Admiralty, to be told: 'There's an unexploded mine on the main Charing Cross railway line right in the middle of Hungerford Bridge.'

The bridge over the Thames linked Charing Cross station with Waterloo East, and still stands today. Some trains and railway sleepers were already on fire from the raid, and the Charing Cross Hotel had been hit, too. The underground trains to and from Waterloo had been stopped for safety reasons and nearby buildings evacuated.

Gidden hurried into an official car, which stopped on the Embankment below Hungerford Bridge. The railway lines were all electrified and the mine managed to fuse itself to a conductor rail before the current had been switched off.

Row upon row of railway carriages were lined up in Charing Cross station. The vital bridge was at a standstill. Big Ben glistened in spring sunshine. Waterloo Bridge stood white against this morning light. St. Paul's, too, was unbowed over to the north-east.

Gidden found the mine squarely across the live electric line. 'The Live Line' was what the Southern Railway used to call it before the war. Unluckily for him, the mine fuse primer release mechanism faced down, away from him and thus impossible to tackle. The mine would have to be rolled over or otherwise shifted before the sensitive clockwork fuse could be seen, let alone handled. The snag was that the slightest shift of this mechanism might fire the whole mine. After a lot of physical strain, and mental stress, Gidden eased the mine over a little, and then some more.

Gidden succeeded in prising a large piece of molten metal from the fuse and then aimed to shove a gag in it to prevent it from springing to life. But the gag could not be forced to fit, as he had hoped. The irregular form of the molten metal precluded it.

The lieutenant had tried things the delicate way. Now he had to resort to sheer strength with a hammer and chisel. Time was passing in a dream, or nightmare. Gidden could not render the mine safe until it was clear of the railway line; a crucial artery to and from the heart of London.

He gave the mine a tentative tap. He listened acutely. There was no whirr to warn him of sudden activity within the mechanism. He tapped a little harder. Still quiet. It was difficult to hear anyway in the river breeze. Another tap, and another. Then a fourth. Slowly the mine and its mechanism edged clear. Finally Gidden got the whole thing free from its fusion to the electric line. The rest was comparatively routine. He rendered it safe. The whole thing had taken a total of six hours. Naturally he could have been blown up at any time. But Charing Cross station, Hungerford Bridge, and the routes to south-east England were open again.

In the course of his matchless career, Ernest Gidden was awarded the George Cross, George Medal, and the OBE.

Charles Henry George Howard,
EARL OF SUFFOLK AND BERKSHIRE

As a research officer in the Ministry of Supply, Lord Suffolk led a scientific research experimental unit. The duties of this group were to look into ways of dismantling and disposing of bombs which had not gone off on impact with the ground, whether intentionally or otherwise.

Lord Suffolk had a vehicle specially fitted with whatever equipment he needed for his role. Together with a driver and secretary, he was ready to travel to any reported case of an unexploded bomb. This practical first-hand experience provided him with evidence to help combat the varied circuitry of enemy bombs. Some of these could include anti-stripping booby traps, while others might involve fresh means of enhancing the effects of terror on the British population by delayed-action or similar devices. Suffolk's job was then to try to devise ways of countering these threats.

ZUS40 was the nomenclature given to a particularly complex booby trap that faced Suffolk. The aim of this trap was to be attached to one end of the fuse, so that if a bomb disposal unit should extract the fuse, this in turn would set off the bomb's charge automatically. Suffolk's answer to this hazard was to incise the bomb casing and thus get rid of the entire apparatus of fuse and ZUS40 without separating the two, with its result of firing the bomb.

Another refinement which superseded this technique was to steam out the whole explosive charge with a pressurized jet. Although this proved an inevitably time-consuming process, it was successful in its purpose and saved many people who would have otherwise perished. The idea could be adapted to landmines as well as bombs, provided that sound was not a factor in the firing circuit equation of the weapon; in other words, not an acoustic mine. These will come to light later on.

The climax to the work of Lord Suffolk and his small staff came on 12 May 1941. They recovered an old mine from a weapons dump, and transported it to the remote area of Erith Marshes for investigation. Despite this being a comparatively ancient and apparently harmless weapon, Suffolk took his customary care in handling it. Together with his staff of two, he had disposed of numerous such bombs and mines over the preceding period of many months. At some stage of the dismantling, and for some reason, the bomb blew up. Lord Suffolk and his faithful helpers were all killed instantly.

Lieutenant Hugh Randall Syme,
ROYAL AUSTRALIAN NAVAL VOLUNTEER RESERVE

Daylight meant death. Or it could have done for Lieutenant Syme, Australian officer from Victoria. Did it mean death for him? He served for a year and three-quarters with the HMS *Vernon* Enemy Mining Section. He tackled an average of one mine per month during this time. As in all operations of this nature, any one of them could have been fatal. This was especially true, since Syme handled a variety of ingenious enemy mines – magnetic, acoustic and magnetic/acoustic.

Sometimes these mines would be laid at sea as intended. Sometimes, however, they might be dropped just over land by mistake. Then one more devilish device appeared at this stage of the war to prevent their being rendered safe and their secrets found. For, of course, this immediately helped to devise antidotes to the enemy mines if their exact mechanisms were known.

So called George mines contained what was by 22 May 1941 a highly advanced idea. Beneath a dome at the rear end of the mine lurked a pair of photoelectric cells, which would set off the whole mine if stimulated by light. This was the latest anti-disposal device to try to keep the mine's magnetic and acoustic properties secret. As well as other precautions, all digging and dealing with it had to be done at night.

It was dusk when Syme reached Pembroke Dock in Wales. In a balloon barrage field nearby, the RAF kept a respectful watch on the mine. 1,500 pounds of explosive slumbered sullenly below ground level. One of the biggest weapons yet used in the war; nearly three-quarters of a ton, and enough to shake the surrounding RAF station.

After examining the thing, Syme said to the station commander: 'I've brought some non-magnetic spades and other gear which we'll want. Shall we say 0930 in the morning, and I hope by dark we'll have it exposed enough for me to tackle the mechanism without risk of getting any light to it.'

It was a mild May morning, though rather oppressive. All went to plan and the manual labour was completed during the forenoon. 'I'll wait till midnight before I start,' Syme told the station commander. 'It's best to let the night set in. This is the plan I propose. As the mine is close to your huts, I'll have to ask you to provide alternative accommodation for the men tonight, in case of accidents. It shouldn't take too long,' Syme went on. 'If you could rig up a telephone, I'll keep in touch with you. Just a routine precaution.'

It was ten to twelve and pitch-black. The night seemed stifling. The wires of the barrage balloons faded into the sky, giving no hint of what floated on their ends. Seventy degrees Fahrenheit, as Syme's watch moved on to midnight.

I'd better take my watch off,' he said to the RAF officer. 'Will you keep it for me?'

The station commander replied: 'Here's your field phone. Just walk out with it and the wire will unwind. I'll be at the other end all the time if you want anything. Best of luck.'

Syme strolled over to the mine, leaving the trail of field phone wire behind him. He adjusted the phone. He was on his own now. 4 a.m: He whispered into the phone, 'I'm taking the nuts off now.

46

One . . . two . . . fourteen . . . twenty-two . . .' The minutes ticked by, tortoise-like, punctuated only by the bald statement of the number of nuts unscrewed.

'Last nut now, I'll get to the photoelectric cell in a moment' Far off he heard a faint rumble. They all asaumed it was another raid somewhere – a long way off.

'Nuts all off. Won't be long now.'

Syme eased the large manganese steel dome away from the body of the mine. In the wan light, he could scarcely see the far side of the dome. He felt around its rim with his fingers, and pressed, eased it off slowly, taking care not to shake the shell of the mine more than he could help. In a second or two, he found himself standing upright with the dome in his hands. He laid it down on the grass. He felt hot, despite the night air. 'Dome removed,' he breathed over the phone. 'I'm just going to wipe my hands. They seem to be sweating. Then I'll get at the switch-gear. I shan't be a second. Don't want to leave it too long. The photo-cells are wide open to the night now. It's come over dark. Look at that cloud,' he added, as he dried his hands on a cloth.

'You should be safe on a night like this, anyway,' came the voice of the RAF officer.

'I'm going to unscrew the switch-gear now. Got to break both circuits before the cells are safe.'

Suddenly, as he spoke, from out of nowhere, an almighty flash filled the sky. Then another and another. The black clouds spat lightning into the night. Syme stood stock still, silhouetted beneath a blaze of light. His rugged frame rooted to the spot. No use running. Wait for it to pass – no choice. Every flash seemed a blow below the belt. Then the thunder rolled around the field. The grass quivered slightly under his feet.

Syme stood his ground. Another fierce fork slashed the sky. It was as light as day for a semi-second. The mine sat still. A barrage balloon burned at the other end of the town. Then a final flash of lightning. The storm died as instantly as it had come. Syme was alive.

Dark again. He breathed again. Sixty seconds or so it had lasted. He did not remember breathing once in that time. He did recall the rumble they had heard a while earlier – thunder.

47

That must have been brewing for quite a time,' he said over the phone. But the RAF officer had not heard. He was running as hard as he could to see Syme.

Back at HMS *Vernon* the scientists pronounced their verdict on the Pembroke Dock mine; the lightning just did not last long enough at a stretch to operate the photoelectric cells and the whole mine circuit, otherwise . . .

Syme won the George Cross not for this particular deed, but another one when he was to be seen 'hanging head downwards in a hole in mud' while doing his dismantling drill.

Corporal James Hendry,
ROYAL CANADIAN ENGINEERS

The Canadians came over to help Britain early in the Second World War. Before he joined the Army, Corporal Hendry had been a miner of considerable experience, so was well suited to be a member of a tunnelling company in the Corps of Royal Canadian Engineers. Hendry found himself posted to Scotland, his actual country of birth, where he was assigned the job of helping to build a tunnel. He was by Loch Laggam in Inverness-shire on 13 June 1941.

When Hendry emerged from the workings at about teatime, he discovered the explosive powder house ablaze. He thought quickly and called to tell the compressor men and steel sharpeners of the emergency. They were in the engineers' workplace. Hendry then ran to make an attempt to extinguish the fire on his own.

He was thinking at once of the catastrophic consequences if the fire spread to the magazine. At this point, Hendry had the time and the opportunity to run clear of any further danger. As in so many cases of emergencies, this was the moment of decision.

Hendry thought he ought to do anything he could to avert the dangerous situation becoming lethal for other men close to the scene. He was cognisant of the imminent odds on an explosion. But he stayed to warn everyone in the proximity to run clear. His gamble was premeditated, but he took it. Most of the men made a successful escape from the carnage of the inevitable eruption, though several were still near enough to be injured by the blast.

Hendry himself and one other of his colleagues did not survive, but his sacrifice had unquestionably resulted in the number of fatalities not numbering more than these two men.

Bombardier Henry Herbert Reed,
ROYAL ARTILLERY

The war at sea. Over the hours of 20–21 June 1941 , the steamship *Cormount* was in a convoy between Blyth and London, when she was attacked by enemy E-boats and aircraft. The attack came from cannon, machine guns and bombs. Although hit amidships under the navigating bridge, the *Cormount*'s crew replied at once with her defensive armament. The men at the guns went on firing, through a hail of bullets and cannon shells.

Bombardier Reed sustained a bad wound early on, but stayed at his anti-aircraft gun. The ship's master repeatedly asked how he was, but Reed replied, 'I'll carry on, sir.' Also wounded had been the chief officer. Already in a weakened condition from his own injuries, Reed somehow carried the officer from the bridge, down two steep ship's ladders, to the deck below and placed him in a shelter near a lifeboat.

Gunner Reed died immediately after this act of astounding gallantry. Later it was found that machine-gun bullets had ripped open the Bombardier's stomach, so that bearing the chief officer from the bridge to safety must have entailed unimaginable effort and pain on his part. Reed was buried in his home county of Durham.

Squadron Leader, the Reverend Herbert Cecil Pugh,
ROYAL AIR FORCE VOLUNTEER RESERVE

A fortnight later came another act at sea, comparable in courage. After seeing war service in Britain, the Reverend Herbert Pugh was posted to Takoradi. He embarked on the troop transport *Anselm* carrying over 1,300 passengers, for West Africa at the end

49

of June 1941. In the early hours of 5 July, the *Anselm* was torpedoed in the Atlantic.

One torpedo hit a hold on Deck C, destroying the normal means of escape. Pugh came up on deck in a dressing gown and gave all the help he could. To an eyewitness on board the *Anselm*, 'he seemed to be everywhere at once', doing his best to comfort the injured and helping with lifeboats and rafts. Two of these were put out of use as a result of the attack. Pugh also went down to the different lower sections of the ship where the men were quartered.

As soon as he learned that some injured airmen were trapped in the damaged hold, he insisted on being lowered into it on a rope. Onlookers demurred, as the hold was clearly below the waterline. Already the decks were awash, and to descend into the hold meant certain death. Pugh said: 'I must be where my men are.'

The deck level was already caving in and the hold was three parts full of water. When he knelt to pray with the men, the water was seen to reach his shoulders. Within a few minutes, the ship continued to settle, before it finally plunged and sank. Pugh was never seen again. He had every opportunity of saving his own life, but in the best tradition of the Royal Air Force and a Christian minister, he chose to die with his men.

Lieutenant Commander William Ewart Hiscock,
ROYAL NAVY

William Hiscock first entered the Royal Navy as long ago as 1900, when he was a mere boy of fourteen. After his retirement in the 1930s, the war resulted in his recall. His posting to Malta meant accepting the responsibility for handling enemy mines which might be laid in and around the vital sea lanes and harbours of the island.

Malta has more than one haven, although the Grand Harbour is, of course, the largest, most important and best known. Hiscock carried out his work quietly and efficiently. In September 1941 the fifty-five-year-old Lieutenant Commander got the job of tackling a fresh menace; the Italian torpedo machine.

One of these unknown quantities had been seen to be dropped in St George's Bay on the island. As it lay in fifteen feet of water, Hiscock had to handle a triple problem; first, of recovering it; second, of rendering it harmless and third, of discovering its exact workings for future reference.

As with all enemy weapons, there could be booby traps which could not be seen by anyone approaching them. Hiscock had to operate with no knowledge of the mechanism which would trigger the machine; no one knew what sort of circuitry had been selected. And as usual, nothing could be ruled in or out when it came actually to the moment of dismantling. Hiscock and another of his naval support staff commenced their task. Clockwork mechanism was heard faintly from within. The two men looked at each other and then went on with the process. A combination of courage and experience rewarded them. There were no further alarms. They dismantled the torpedo machine safely.

Lieutenant Commander Hiscock never knew that he had won the George Cross. He died on Malta five months later and it was June 1942 before the *London Gazette* announced the award for his crucial work on Malta.

Leading Aircraftman Karl Mander Gravell,
ROYAL CANADIAN AIR FORCE

Swedish-born Karl Gravell joined the Royal Canadian Air Force early in the war and was on an aircrew course at Calgary in Alberta during the autumn of 1941. Early in November, Gravell was flying while under wireless telegraphy instruction when the training aeroplane actually crashed. Despite the severity of the impact, Gravell clawed a way clear of the burning aircraft. Although the crash caused great shock to him – plus his being blinded in one of his eyes and in agony from fire burns – he instinctively realized that the pilot was still trapped.

Gravell groped back towards the pilot in a vain effort to rescue him, but the vicious conflagration swept around him. Gravell was himself rescued, but his burns proved too advanced and he died from them. If he had thought first of himself and not of his colleague, he might well have survived. So irrespective or not of whether he was successful, this was still a case of supreme self-sacrifice.

Lieutenant George Herbert Goodman,
ROYAL NAVAL VOLUNTEER RESERVE

Mines and torpedoes were always closely connected – in development, manufacture and service. HMS *Vernon* was, in fact, the base for both of these types of weapons. Inevitably, perhaps, the need for rendering them safe occurred far more frequently with mines than torpedoes.

Lieutenant Goodman was one of the few officers decorated for gallantry when handling enemy torpedoes, though he also became experienced in enemy mines as well. On Christmas Eve, 1941, the focus for George Cross awards swung to the eastern Mediterranean, where Goodman was responsible for stripping the very first so-called 'Sammy' mine found in that theatre of the war.

However, it was just three weeks later, on 15 January 1942, that Goodman was really recognized and recommended for the George Cross. The North African coast and control of it proved crucial in the Desert War. On that date, Goodman got the unenviable task of facing only the second example of an Italian self-destruct surface torpedo to come into Allied hands along that coast.

Goodman went to work in the ultimately uncomfortable knowledge that only a matter of days earlier, the first similar torpedo found had been approached by the HMS *Medway* torpedo officer and his support team. The weapon went off and killed them all . . .

Goodman saw the second such torpedo. Now he knew it was dangerous and could kill. But he also knew the background facts to the previous attempt to render the weapon safe. He went ahead and overcame the triple menace of three detonating pistols – and also succeeded in parting strikers from their primers and detonators. Fortunately for him, the self-destruct ability of the torpedo was defeated and the secrets of the whole weapon laid bare by him.

Lieutenant George Goodman was awarded the George Cross in September 1942, but a tragic postscript was added when he died near Rotterdam soon after the end of the war in Europe.

Chapter Three

1942

On 15 April 1942, the whole island of Malta was awarded the George Cross. The letter, sent by King George VI to the Governor of Malta said:

> To honour her brave people I award the GeorgeCross to the Island Fortress of Malta to bear witness to a heroism and devotion that will long be famous in history.

So the George Cross was bestowed, first and foremost, to the Maltese people themselves. Yet their ordeal was played out against the dramatic backdrop of warfare by air, sea and under the sea. Convoys to Malta helped the island survive, while the Royal Navy's Malta submarines wrote their own saga by sinking enemy shipping en route to North Africa.

From the viewpoint of the Maltese inhabitants themselves, however, the British Army and Royal Air Force probably came into closest contact with what they endured; attack from the air. So this account concentrates on the island of Malta, her people and Allied services stationed there.

The stakes of the struggle were for possession of Malta and control of the Mediterranean. It was as basic as that, with the island the crucial key. If it fell, the whole North African campaign could be lost.

From June 1940 to November 1942, the island had 3,215 air-raid warnings; an average of one every seven hours for two-and-a-half years. The enemy dropped 14,000 tons of bombs, killed 1,468 Maltese civilians, destroyed or damaged 24,000 buildings and lost 1,129 aircraft.

When the battle began on 10 June 1940, the date Italy entered the war, the defence of Malta rested on three Gladiator biplanes which became known as Faith, Hope and Charity. For three weeks, this trio took on the full weight of the Italian air force sent to crush the island.

At the end of June, however, four Hurricanes arrived and throughout July these seven fighters alone faced about 200 enemy aircraft operating from Sicily. Raids were carried out almost every day. The defence was so fierce that eventually the Italians, despite their enormous superiority in numbers, only ventured over the island by night. The British losses were one Hurricane and one Gladiator.

On 2 August 1940, HMS *Argus* steamed within 200 miles of Malta to fly off twelve Hurricanes and two Skuas. This consignment arrived safely and formed the basis for a more effective fighter defence of the island and her people. During August the enemy turned from the dockyards to the airfields, attempting to smash Malta's first line of defence. Then the Italians brought in German dive-bombers, Junkers 87s. Twenty of these attacked the Hal Far airfield on 15 September, dropping delayed-action bombs. But it was the arrival of the Luftwaffe on Sicilian airfields that marked a grimmer stage in the long battle.

On 17 November, twelve more Hurricanes were embarked on HMS *Argus*. The Italian fleet forced the carrier to put about at the Hurricanes' extreme range from Malta. Out of twelve Hurricanes and two Skuas, only four Hurricanes and one Skua reached Luqa, Malta. The rest ran out of fuel. It was a costly error.

Soon afterwards, the aircraft carrier HMS *Illustrious* steamed into Grand Harbour with a convoy. She was listing and badly down by the stern. During the next few hours, the sirens sounded for enemy reconnaissance planes several times. The people waited for the inevitable attack: Hurricanes and naval Fulmar fighters waited as well. The plan to defend the *Illustrious* was to put up a fierce anti-aircraft barrage, creating a curtain of fire over the harbour. The dive-bombers would have to fly through this to reach their targets. Between 1 p.m. and 2.45 p.m. over seventy aircraft came in.

As the barrage began, Malta had never heard such a noise, and it was amplified by the guns of the ships in the harbour. The fighters waited to catch the enemy as they came in and later as they banked away from Grand Harbour. Sometimes the fighters followed the enemy in through the barrage. Two hundred houses were wiped out by the raid and 500 damaged. The church clock of Our Lady of Victories pointed to 2.20 p.m. for the rest of the war, a reminder of that fierce afternoon of 16 January 1941. But the carrier *Illustrious* was still there.

Two days later, eighty dive-bombers attacked the airfields at Luqa and Hal Far in an attempt to engage and reduce the number of fighters defending the *Illustrious*. For a time, Luqa went out of action. The island's striking forces became badly depleted, but the few fighter pilots shot down seven enemy aircraft, while four more went to ground gunners.

Next day, 19 January, the Germans again attacked the Grand Harbour. Six Hurricanes, one Fulmar and a Gladiator met them. The fighters shot down eleven, the guns eight, and the surviving raiders retreated. On 23 January, the *Illustrious* escaped, two days later she was safe in Alexandria.

In February 1941 began the second German assault from the air. The enemy made large-scale minelaying raids on the harbours and creeks. On 17 February, the island had raids for the eleventh night in succession, yet the harbour remained effective. The people were taking it, just as they were in the London and British Blitz.

The pilots of the small Hurricane force were losing a lot of sleep, while still having to face the sweeps of Messerschmitt 109s. On 16 February, two enemy formations came over Malta. The Me 109s split up on sighting the Hurricanes, one formation climbing above, the other dropping below. Flight Lieutenant J.A.F. McLachlan led a Hurricane flight and described the experience:

While on patrol over Luqa at 20,000 feet, we were attacked from above and astern by six Me 109s. As previously arranged, the flight broke away to the right and formed a defensive circle. As I took my place in the circle, I saw four more Me 109s coming out of the sun. Just as they came within range, I turned back towards them and they all over-shot me without firing. I looked very carefully but could see no more enemy aircraft above me, so I turned back to the tail of the nearest Me 109. I was turning well inside him and was just about to open fire when I was hit in the left arm by a cannon shell. My dashboard was completely smashed so I baled out and landed safely by parachute.

MacLachlan's left arm was amputated at Imtarfa Hospital. When he came out, a colleague flew him round in a Magister. Then he took off by himself and landed faultlessly. A few days later, he flew a Hurricane and asked to rejoin his squadron. Back in Britain he had an artificial arm fitted and flew on many more successful operations.

The statistics of this battle for Malta were sensational. Since the outbreak of war, the few fighters there had claimed as many as ninety-six aircraft destroyed for the loss of sixteen fighters and eleven pilots. But the enemy was slowly gaining an upper hand and flying lower and lower, neutralizing the striking power of the air defence. In the course of ten days nearly all the RAF flight leaders were lost. At the beginning of March 1941, an official signal reported:

Blitz raid of several formations totalling certainly no less than 100 aircraft, of which at least 60 bombers, attacked Hal Far. A few of these aircraft dropped bombs and machine-gunned Kalafranca. Damage at Kalafranca was slight both to buildings and aircraft. One Sunderland unserviceable for a few days. Damage Hal Far still being assessed.
    Preliminary report as follows: three Swordfish and one Gladiator burnt out. All other aircraft temporarily unservice-able. All barrack blocks unserviceable and one demolished. Water and power cut off. Hangars considerably damaged. Airfield temporarily unserviceable. Eleven fighters up. Enemy casualties by our fighters, two Ju 99s, two Ju 87s, one Do 215, two Me 109s, confirmed. One Ju 88 and three Ju 87s damaged. By AA, one Me 110 and eight other aircraft

confirmed, also four damaged. One Hurricane and one pilot lost after first shooting down one Ju 87 included above.

For the blitz every serviceable Hurricane and every available pilot was put up and they achieved results against extremely heavy odds. The only answer to this kind of thing is obviously more fighters and these must somehow be provided if the air defence of Malta is to be maintained.

The raids did not decrease, but towards the end of April another twenty-three Hurricanes arrived. A month later, more Hurricanes flew in and about June the Luftwaffe left Sicily for the Russian front. Even so, the battle for Malta was not yet over.

Six months passed. At the beginning of 1942 the Luftwaffe returned for the kill. The island was becoming increasingly important on the sea supply route for the North African campaign in which Britain was locked in a life or death struggle with Rommel.

In March the onslaught was at its height. Spitfires flew in from the aircraft carrier *Eagle*. There were fifteen of them. It was planned to employ them in sections of six or four against the bombers. An RAF sergeant manning a fire tender on one of the airfields described that day:

The Spitfires came waggling their wings as if to say 'O.K., boys, we're here.' But that very same evening the gen went round that a big plot was building up over Sicily and within half an hour or so we were to see that Jerry really meant business. Standing at a vantage point in the village of Zurrieq, I saw the first waves of 88s coming all the way over the island. They dived down on Takali where the whole batch of Spits had landed. We tried to count them as they came in, but it was an utter impossibility. Straight down they went, and one could see the stuff leave the kites before it really got dark.

The guns were belting rounds up like nothing on earth; tracers filled the sky, and if things weren't so serious one could have called it a lovely sight. The din was terrific and Takali seemed to be ablaze from end to end. The lads would shout that some gun or other had stopped firing, and the crew had been knocked out. But no; they started again pushing up rounds harder than ever. This time Jerry seemed to be under orders to finish the place and, by hell, he tried his best.

Despite more raids for the rest of the week, the Spitfires were up in action within three days and had destroyed their first aircraft. But their presence attracted more enemy attacks.

By 24 April, a single section of Spitfires was fully operational. Meanwhile the Germans realized that they could not advance in the desert without getting through supplies from Europe to North Africa. But Malta threatened their convoy routes. For that reason, air power was concentrated in Sicily to try to neutralize the island. If Malta had not held out, these aeroplanes would have been diverted elsewhere.

During April 1942, 6,728 tons of bombs fell on Malta. The dockyards received nearly half, and the three airfields of Luqa, Takali and Hal Far most of the rest. The people suffered, too, 300 being killed in April alone, with over 10,000 buildings destroyed or damaged. On an average, 170 bombers came over every day, Ju 88s and 87s attacking in waves of twelve to fifteen at a few minute intervals. Three raids a day became typical: the total time spent under alert in April was twelve days ten hours and twenty minutes.

One Hurricane squadron had been re-equipped with Spitfires, while a second was converted in April. But many Spitfires were lost on the ground, and it was, once more, the Hurricanes that bore the strain of the battle. Sometimes a dozen Hurricanes would take off to meet a raid of 100 enemy aircraft. Often the odds grew greater. An RAF corporal wrote:

During dinner time the Hun started again. This time he dropped quite a number of bombs on Luqa village. A direct hit was scored on a shelter. It appeared that water was seeping into the shelter drowning the people trapped there. The Army and RAF squads were attempting to get through to them. After tea another raid – bombs all over the place. As I am writing, the 6 p.m. news from Blighty can be heard in the sergeants' mess. It makes me just a little homesick . . .

Malta at bay. Under the fury of attack, men went out to their work, women tended their homes, the dive-bombers blasted the island, and the RAF also struggled on. But by the middle of April, the fighter defence was seriously weakened. The defenders thought themselves lucky if they could put up half a dozen aircraft regularly; four to engage the enemy and two for airfield defence. The system used was to scramble the four strikers immediately the warning was received. 'Scramble . . . Scramble . . . Hostile aircraft approaching . . .'

The fighters would then gain height as rapidly as they could into the sun. To save petrol, the airfield defence pair became airborne at the latest possible moment. Keeping radio silence, they flew to a point twenty to thirty miles south of the island. There they gained height until ordered by radio to swoop to whichever airfield was most in need of defence.

During those days of April, the Malta pilots even fought without ammunition! The Germans were never sure when they were really without it but such was their reputation that the enemy always sheered off just in case they had it.

Ingenuity played its part. April was the month that Pilot Officer 'Humgufery' appeared on the scene. He was the brainchild of Group Captain A.B. Woodhall, the remarkable controller in charge of the Malta operations room. On one occasion, all our fighters were grounded to try and increase serviceability. The enemy happened to come over in force with quite a large fighter cover. There were several fighter pilots with Woodhall in the ops room at the time, one a Canadian. Woodhall put him at the microphone of a stand-by radio set and proceeded to give him dummy orders. He replied just as if he were flying his fighter! This caused a cry of 'Achtung! Schpitfeuer' to go over the Germans' own radio, and two Me 109s actually shot each other down without any British aircraft being airborne.

It was on 15 April that the whole island of Malta was awarded the George Cross. On 20 April, Spitfires flew in from the American aircraft carrier *Wasp*. They were virtually chased in, forty-seven reaching the island out of an original fifty-four aircraft. The moment they arrived an attack was launched against them on the ground. While they were still being refuelled, rearmed and serviced, many of them were 'spitchered'. The enemy sent over 300 bombers in one day to destroy them. By the end of the next day, only eighteen were serviceable, and within three days of landing, every single Spitfire had been grounded.

Although the enemy lost nearly 200 aircraft in April, the RAF fared worse than usual by comparison, with twenty-three Spitfires lost and fifty-seven damaged, and eighteen Hurricanes lost and thirty damaged. Air raids went on and on. Fighters became fewer. Then the enemy made the fatal blunder of easing up for a few days at the end of the month. Sixty-four Spitfires got through to land on the airfields from 1 a.m. on Saturday 9 May. These had flown off the USS *Wasp* and HMS *Eagle*.

But the RAF had to be careful not to lose them on the ground before they could go into action. Wing Commander E.J. Gracie wrote:

We went to our pilots and ground crew and administrative staffs and told them we were going to give them, we hoped, an organisation which would enable us to win the Battle of Malta, which at that time we were in grave danger of losing. We then told them it would mean the hardest possible work under very difficult conditions; and that we were going to enlist the aid of the Army, both in men and materials, but that the battle was lost unless they all pulled their weight one hundred per cent.

The response was tremendous. Every man felt himself an important item in the battle and not merely an insignificant unit. So magnificently did the ground staffs work that our half-hour service became an absolute outside limit, and the official records show that six Spitfires of one squadron took off to engage the enemy within nine minutes of landing on the island. What a change in 36 hours! Within half an hour, every serviceable Spitfire was in the air. I shall never forget the remark of one airman who, coming out of a slit trench, and seeing two or three squadrons in the air, said 'Heavens, look at the fog!

In some cases the Spitfires were actually turned round in six minutes. When the enemy came to try to bomb them on the ground, the Luftwaffe were met and attacked by these same aeroplanes in the air. On the ground, each Spitfire was met and directed by a runner to a dispersal pen. Owing to the shortage of petrol bowsers, and all the aircraft having to be refuelled virtually at once, petrol supplies were stored in tins for refuelling by hand. These tins, together with oil, glycol and ammunition, were waiting ready in each pen.

All day long, ground crews, pilots and relief pilots lived in these pens. Army wireless sets, dispatch riders and signalmen kept touch among them all. And all day long, too, repair squads were dashing out filling up bomb craters on the runways, while the bombers which had made them were flying back to Sicily. One of the new Spitfire pilots described his first day:

Took off from the *Wasp* at 0645 hours. Landed at Takali at 1030 hours. The formation leader flew too fast and got the navigation all to hell, so I left them 40 miles west of Bizerta, five miles off the North African coast, and set course for Malta, avoiding Pantellaria and Bizerta owing to fighters and flak being present there. Jettisoned the long-range tank 20 miles west of Bizerta and reached Malta with twenty gallons to spare in main tank. Of the forty-seven machines that flew off the *Wasp*, one crashed into the sea on take-off, one force-landed back on to the deck as he had jettisoned his auxiliary tank in error, one landed in Algeria, one ran out of petrol between Pantellaria and Malta, one crashed on landing at Hal Far, and one crashed off Grand Harbour.

On landing at Takali I immediately removed my kit, and the machine was rearmed and refuelled. I landed during a raid and four Me 109s tried to shoot me up. Soon after landing, the airfield was bombed but without much damage being done. I was scrambled in a section of four soon after the raid, but we failed to intercept the next one, though we chased several 109s down on the deck. Ate lunch in the aircraft as I was at the ready till dusk. After lunch we were heavily bombed again by eight Ju 88s.

Scrambled again in the same section after tea – no luck again. One Spit was shot down coming in to land and another one at the edge of the airfield. Score for the day, seven confirmed, seven probables and fourteen damaged for the loss of three Spits.

The tempo of life here is just indescribable. The morale of all is magnificent - pilots, ground crew and Army, but life is certainly tough. The bombing is continuous on and off all day. One lives here only to destroy the Hun and hold him at bay; everything else, living conditions, sleep, food, and all the ordinary standards of life have gone by the board. It all makes the Battle of Britain and fighter sweeps seem like child's play in comparison, but it is certainly history in the making, and nowhere is there aerial warfare to compare with this.

There were nine air raids that day. The 'fog' of Spitfires began to show results within hours. Eight enemy planes were destroyed, plus many probables. A shock of excitement and exultation shivered through everyone.

The next day was destined to be another milestone for Malta: the climax of the battle if not its end. The minelaying cruiser HMS *Welshman*, capable of forty knots, was due to berth in Grand Harbour soon after dawn. The enemy would be sure to try to sink her. At 5.45 a.m. an alert sounded, but it was no more than an enemy reconnaissance. The Luftwaffe came in force that day. But the Germans were due for no fewer than three shocks – a smokescreen, a blistering barrage and squadrons of Spitfires. All these precautions were necessary as the cruiser carried a cargo mainly of ammunition, which was unloaded in five hours.

Smoke containers were brought ashore first, and these augmented the smoke generators in use for the first time in Grand Harbour. The smokescreen was started at a signal from the fighter ops room. The harbour area had overall priority for the gun barrage, specially sited to cover the cruiser. The RAF fighters were warned that the barrage would continue regardless of their whereabouts.

10.56 a.m. – the heaviest raid of the day. Twenty Stukas and ten Ju 88s came escorted by Me 109s. The enemy dived as low as they dared, dropping some forty tons of bombs over the Grand Harbour zone. One was a near miss for the *Welshman* still being unloaded.

Thirty-seven Spitfires and thirteen Hurricanes went up to intercept; fifty fighters, an unheard of number. As the first wave of Ju 88s dived out of the sun, the fighters were already 'mixing it' with them. Combats developed all over the sky. Then the Ju 87s sailed in from the east. The harbour barrage erupted and the Spitfires jumped on them, many Spits following Stukas through their own barrage.

In the afternoon came another attack, but by then the ship had unloaded its cargo. The same drill met the raiders; smoke, fire and fighters. The evening brought a two-wave raid, first a high-level attack by Cant 1007s and then Stukas.

The same pilot who described his first day on Malta had this to say about the second:

We climbed to 4,000 feet, and then the barrage was put up by the harbour defences and the cruiser. The C.O. dived down into it and I followed close on him. We flew three times to and fro in the barrage, trusting to luck to avoid the flak. Then I spotted a Ju 87 climbing out of the fringe of the barrage and I turned and chased him. I gave him a one-second burst of cannon and he broke off sharply to the left. At that moment another Ju 87 came up in front of my nose and I turned into him and I let him have it. His engine started to pour out black smoke and he started weaving. I kept the button pushed hard, and after a further two- or three-second burst with the one cannon I had left, the other having jammed, he keeled over at 1,500 feet and went into the drink.

I then spotted a 109 firing at me from behind and pulled the kite round to port, and after one and a half turns got on his tail. Before I could fire, another 109 cut across my bows from the port side and I turned straight on his tail and fired, till my cannon stopped through lack of ammo. He was hit and his engine poured out black smoke, but I had to beat it as I was now defenceless and two more 109s were attacking me.

I spiralled straight down to the sea at full throttle, and I then weaved violently toward the land with the two 109s still firing at me. I went under the fringe of the smokescreen to try to throw them off, but when I came out the other side I found them both sitting up top waiting for me. I therefore kept right down at nought feet steep-turned towards them, noticing the smoke from their gun ports as I did so. After about five minutes of this, I managed to throw them off. I landed back at Takali and made out my report, claiming an 87 destroyed and one Me 109 damaged.

There were 110 Spitfire sorties and fourteen Hurricane sorties on that day, 10 May 1942. They destroyed fifteen attackers, and ack-ack shot down a further eight. Three Spitfires were lost, but two of the pilots saved, so that *Welshman* had been protected from enemy air attack for the loss of one pilot. After that the Germans made fewer daylight raids but more by night. Their losses were still substantial.

June saw the arrival on the Malta scene of one of the most unusual aces of all, George 'Screwball' Beurling. A real lone-wolf fighter pilot from Canada, Beurling disliked discipline and routine. Not surprisingly, therefore, he had had a chequered if colourful career by the time he joined 249 Squadron on the island.

He started scoring seriously on 6 July and in a matter of a few weeks Screwball became the top-notch pilot of the entire Malta campaign. One of his eccentricities was that he had been offered a commission on several occasions, but had refused to take it. Eventually, at some stage that year, he was simply informed that he had been commissioned!

After bringing down many of the enemy, Screwball Beurling destroyed a Junkers 88 on 14 October 1942, before himself being hit. Despite this, he shot down two more Me 109s before baling out with a wounded heel. He fell into the sea, was rescued, and recovered in hospital. A little later, he was being flown home in a Liberator when it crashed into the sea while trying to land at

Gibraltar. The aircraft broke in half, but Beurling was one of the few to survive, breaking a leg. Later in the war, he flew again in the European theatre. He died on 20 May 1948 while piloting a Mitchell aircraft to Israel.

The battle for Malta still raged, but now more in Allied favour. A new plan was introduced, of intercepting enemy bombers before they could reach Malta, and this in time tilted the scales still further. But the inevitable result of this plan was that pilots and aeroplanes were liable to come down in the Mediterranean and so the Air-Sea Rescue Service became more vital than ever. This is a typical story from a high-speed launch log:

At 1100 we had a call out in HSL 128 for a Spitfire pilot, said to have baled out on a bearing of 160 Hal Far, about 100 yards out. Sounded like a piece of cake, for even though enemy fighters were plentiful in the vicinity, the position given was close to the island and we now had Spitfires on the job as well as Hurricanes. Getting on the given bearing, we steamed 100, 200, 300 yards – still nothing to be seen – and kept on going, though enemy activity was getting more and more lively overhead.

After we had steamed out about three miles, one of the escorting Hurricanes was shot down a couple of miles ahead of us. It was while we were investigating this wreckage that Jerry got closest to us, but even then the bullets only churned up the water 100 feet away. As there was no survivor from this crash and still no sign of the original pilot for whom we had been called out, I decided to make for base, but on our way back we saw another fighter crash about six miles over to the westward and a parachute drifting down. We picked this pilot up within a few minutes of his hitting the water, and he turned out to be a Hun – a cheery soul who advised us to get back ashore before we were hurt.

As we were then fairly well out, I decided to run out and then come in on our original bearing from a distance of about ten miles, as even the worst possible estimate of distance could hardly be over ten miles out. We actually found the Spitfire pilot in his dinghy about nine miles from land, and the German pilot insisted upon shaking hands with him as he welcomed him aboard.

Malta was still besieged, short of food, and bombed. The convoys still had to claw their way to and from the island. As late as 11 October 1942, fifty-eight bombers blasted Malta, and during the next week there were nearly 250 raiders by day. But on 23 October came Rommel's defeat, while soon afterwards the Americans invaded from the west. The Allies were soon sweeping across North Africa from both ends. At long last, the siege was raised. The people of Malta deserved their George Cross.

Continuing the Malta story to its end, on 11 September 1943, came this classic signal:

From C in C Mediterranean. To Admiralty 'Be pleased to inform their Lordships that the Italian battlefleet now lies at anchor under the guns of the fortress of Malta.'

Lieutenant Dennis Arthur Copperwheat,
ROYAL NAVY

The setting was still Malta for the first individual George Cross, to be awarded for 1942. The relentlessly heavy enemy air attacks were devastating the precious Allied convoys to Malta over a long period. At the time of one of these, on 22 March 1942, a merchantman lay scorching inside Grand Harbour. The ship was laden with ammunition and so liable to explode and cause disastrous damage to other vessels and to Valletta, the capital of the island.

Lieutenant Copperwheat was sent with a small party from the cruiser HMS *Penelope* to scuttle the merchantman before she could cause such havoc. Owing to the fires and firework-like bursts from stray ammunition, it proved impossible to place the scuttling charges in the holds of the ship. They had to be slung over her side.

As the men continued to work, ammunition went on exploding around them from burning stowages on deck. The ship lay only forty yards from the shore, hence the concern for overall safety afloat and ashore. The electric cables for firing the scuttling charges could only just reach this distance.

Copperwheat sent the others to shelter and stayed himself to fire the charges. In this firing position, he had to be exposed to the full blast of the ensuing explosion, which lifted him bodily. He survived the shock waves, however, and completed the task. Without his action, the merchantman would have blown up and grave damage been done. More than this, much of the ammunition was salvaged and some very heavy bombs, which formed part of the cargo, were actually dropped on Italy soon afterwards.

Leading Aircraftman Albert Matthew Osborne,
ROYAL AIR FORCE

During the fierce air attacks on Malta, Leading Aircraftman Osborne displayed 'unsurpassed courage' ashore, just as Lieutenant Copperwheat had done in Grand Harbour. In circumstances of great personal danger, he was always first at hand, leading his men to deal with a variety of emergencies. These covered firefighting operations and rescue work, including the following nine examples of his promptitude and gallantry:

He rendered safe the torpedo of a burning torpedo aircraft, working a mere three feet from the main tank for ten minutes.

He extinguished a burning aircraft during a heavy bombing attack on Luqa air station.

He attempted to save another burning aircraft and he subsequently removed torpedoes from the dangerous vicinity.

He assisted in saving the pilot of a blazing aircraft and putting out the fire.

He saved yet another aircraft from destruction by fire.

He tried to extricate airmen from a bombed shelter for six hours throughout continuous bombing and danger from falling stonework.

He fought fires in two aircraft, his efforts resulting in the saving of one precious plane.

He freed the parachute of a burning flare caught in an aircraft, enabling the pilot to taxi clear.

He checked the fire in a burning aircraft, the greater part of which was left undamaged. The last three of these incidents occurred on the same day.

Finally, just ten days after Copperwheat's exploit aboard the merchantman, on 1–2 April 1942 he led a rescue party to extinguish the flames of a burning aircraft. This was happening during an intense air assault. Preserving the precious aircraft was crucial to the continued defence and survival of Malta.

As Osborne led his party towards the aircraft, a petrol tank exploded and he was injured as well as being affected by the fumes. On recovery, he insisted on returning to fight the fire. But tragically while he was aiming to pour water over torpedoes in danger of going off, an air vessel went off and killed him. Summing up the catalogue of courage shown by the leading aircraftman the Air Officer Commanding, Royal Air Force Mediterranean, stated that he was 'one of the bravest airmen it has been my privilege to meet'.

Lieutenant John Stuart Mould,
ROYAL AUSTRALIAN NAVAL VOLUNTEER RESERVE

John Mould joined HMS *Vernon* Enemy Mining Section about the same time as fellow Australian Hugh Syme. Mould got his first experience of the photoelectric cells at Milford Haven, near the large wartime mine depot situated there. The main charge of the mine had already fired, but the unit housing the cells and the rest of the circuit had been thrown clear.

'It was fairly plain sailing,' Mould insisted afterwards.

Another seventy-two hours and he was at Belfast, chasing one seven feet down in the ground. Next day, back at Stepney, London, he met Hugh Syme. Together they tackled Mould's third in four days. That was only three days before Syme received his call to Pembroke Dock.

From March 1941, Mould was always in danger. The period cited in his award fell between 14 November 1941 and 30 June 1942. And specifically the citation referred to his successful stripping of the first magnetic-acoustic mine fitted with devices that had resulted in the tragic death of several other officers engaged in rendering safe enemy mines.

Apprentice Donald Owen Clarke,
MERCHANT NAVY

The *San Emiliano* was a tanker sailing out of Trinidad with a lethal cargo of precious petrol. She was about forty-eight hours out of the Caribbean island on 9 August 1942. Suddenly the tanker was ripped by two torpedoes from an unseen U-boat. Fire broke out from bridge to poop.

Apprentice Donald Clarke was trapped in the accommodation quarters and severely burned. Somehow he struggled to reach the deck. He was one of the crew who got into the only lifeboat that left the ship. The small craft was crammed with other crew, also burned from the flames.

The painter of the boat was kept fast and the helm put over and as the vessel still carried some way, it was towed clear of the ship's side. But when they cast off the painter, the lifeboat began to drift back, and it was clear to all on board that it would need a tremendous effort to pull it out of danger. Most of the men were so badly burned that they were unable to help. However, Apprentice Clarke took an oar and pulled heartily for two hours without a word of complaint.

It was not until after the boat was clear that the others realized how badly Clarke had been injured. His hands had to be cut away from the oar, as the burnt flesh stuck to it. He had pulled as well as any of the few others who did manage to row – although he was doing it with the bones of his hands. Later, when lying at the bottom of the boat, his thoughts were still with his shipmates and he sang to help keep up their spirits.

Next day, he died . . .

The citation said:

By his supreme effort, undertaken without thought of self and in spite of terrible agony, Apprentice Clarke ensured the safety of his comrades in the boat. His great heroism and selfless devotion were in keeping with the highest traditions of the Merchant Navy.

Captain Dudley William Mason,
MERCHANT NAVY

Seventy-two hours later came another deed earning the George Cross for a member of the Merchant Navy. Captain Dudley Mason was the British Master of the steamship *Ohio*, a 14,000-ton American tanker – as its name implied. Although belonging to the Texas Oil Company, the vessel was on loan to Britain and formed one of the fourteen ships in a typically important convoy to Malta.

During the passage, the merchant vessels were being escorted by both sea and air, but they began to be attacked on 11 August 1942. By the following day it became clear that the large tanker would be the focus of air and U-boat attack. The ship started to suffer a violent onslaught from the first of the ensuing four days. Early one night, she was torpedoed badly, while two sticks of bombs straddled her, vibrating her whole structure.

Yet another bomb-burst caught her boiler room. Although the *Ohio* was gravely damaged, the crew kept her engines going and the Master made a magnificent passage towards Malta by hand-steering being devoid of any compass. The ship's gunners helped to bring down a Stuka dive-bomber, which actually crashed on the ship's deck. Before morning the *Ohio* sustained more hits, but though she still did not sink, her engine room was wrecked. The order to abandon ship was given twice. Later she was re-boarded

Taken into tow with her precious cargo of fuel, the *Ohio* presented an unwieldy spectacle and continued to be the target of persistent enemy attacks. She made slow progress while under tow and it was uncertain whether she could, or would, remain afloat long enough to make port. Captain Mason played the role of Master with brilliance while all next day the *Ohio* was towed towards Malta.

The tanker crew finally glimpsed the island on 15 August. Throughout the four days they had been subjected almost nonstop to bombs and torpedoes. But this had not deterred Mason from his dedicated purpose of delivering his cargo.

The *Ohio* eventually limped into harbour, lashed between a pair of the escorting destroyers. The priceless fuel was pumped out of her tanks – and then she sank. Throughout the time since the enemy made contact with the convoy, Mason showed skill and courage and it was due to his determination that they finally got through to a safe berth. Mason accepted his GC not only for himself but on behalf of his whole crew. He lived to the age of eighty-five.

Lieutenant William George Foster,
HOME GUARD

Sixty-year-old William Foster was an officer in the 7th Wiltshire (Salisbury) Battalion of the Home Guard. On 13 September 1942, he was on duty at Ashley Hill, Clarendon Park, near his home town of Salisbury.

Foster had a section of new entrants to the Home Guard with him and he was demonstrating to them how to toss a grenade from the security of a defensive trench. The recruits took it in turn to try out the technique. But when it came to one of them, he failed to hurl it far enough, or sufficiently high.

Within sight and range of all the others, including Foster, the live grenade struck the parapet in front of them, seemed to be suspended there and then rolled down into the slit trench, close to all of them. The fuse of the grenade was due to set it off literally at any second, so Lieutenant Foster hurled himself on the weapon.

The eruption killed him on the spot, but by sacrificing himself he had saved the others.

Sergeant Graham Leslie Parish,
ROYAL AIR FORCE VOLUNTEER RESERVE

The setting: an airfield in Anglo-Egyptian Sudan. Thirty-year-old Sergeant Graham Parish was the navigator of a bomber during a delivery flight from Britain to the Middle East Command. The aircraft took off from the airfield on 16 September 1942, but shortly afterwards its port engine failed and the pilot attempted to turn and land on the airfield.

Due to the rough nature of the ground, the pilot could not make full use of the aircraft brakes – with the result that the machine struck a building on the field and burst into flames.

Most of the crew managed to scramble free of the blazing bomber, with the exception of Sergeant Parish and a passenger whose legs were both broken. At the moment of the crash, Parish had been at the bomber's astro-hatch and the passenger at the emergency door in the floor of the fuselage. This door was unusable, however, as the plane's undercarriage had collapsed and its fuselage was resting on the ground. Neither man could be given any assistance as within seconds the fire was so intense that it devoured the bomber.

Since the passenger could not walk, Parish struggled to carry him the eight yards or more from the emergency door to the rear turret, hoping that they could escape this way. Undoubtedly both men must have been overcome by the smoke and flame and burned to death in this heroic attempt at rescue.

When the emergency services on the airfield put out the blaze, Parish's body was found leaning against the rear gun turret, with the passenger beside him, his arm over the navigator's shoulder. Straight after the crash, Sergeant Parish could have escaped through the astro-hatch, his location at the time of impact. But he instinctively and instantly made the decision to try to save the injured passenger. As in so many other instances of awards of the George Cross, this selflessness cost him his life.

73

Lieutenant Francis Anthony Blair Fasson,
ROYAL NAVY
Able Seaman Colin Grazier,
ROYAL NAVY

The scene shifts to the Mediterranean. This story shows that in wartime anything might endanger life at any moment. On 30 October 1942, a German U-boat was spotted, surfaced and unawares, by a British aircraft. The crew of the plane reported her whereabouts to the Royal Navy's Twelfth Destroyer Flotilla, which initiated an immediate search.

After a prolonged period trying to locate the U-boat, the Royal Navy established rough contact and started to depth-charge the area. As in all attacks by depth charge, the purpose was either to destroy the submarine or to drive it to the desperate measure of breaking surface and surrendering.

The charges must have been close enough to the U-boat to inflict a decision to surface on the German captain. The British destroyers at once aimed their guns on the submarine. It was in fact damaged from the depth-charge attack and then the opening of gunfire produced an immediate surrender from the Germans. In strict accordance with traditions and the rules of warfare, the Royal Navy ships saved the U-boat crew and made them prisoners of war.

For Lieutenant Fasson and Able Seaman Grazier, however, that was the start of the story, not its end. If possible, the enemy documentation had to be captured, too. Fasson and Grazier, from HMS *Petard*, boarded the crippled U-boat and started the hazardous search for the enemy papers, instruments and any other items valuable for future intelligence.

But the U-boat had been so severely and terminally hit by the attack that the Mediterranean was infiltrating into her at a rapid rate. Furthermore, all lighting was gone, so they were facing double danger and difficulty. It was clear to them that the submarine would not survive long. Despite this, Fasson and Grazier did not waver. They went on with their duty of transferring all the documents and apparatus they could get hold of in these nightmare surroundings.

Before they could complete the work, suddenly the U-boat started to plunge. With the vast weight of water added to the damage inflicted earlier, the vessel sank with no further warning. Neither Fasson nor Grazier had any chance to abandon her and they went down as well.

Chapter Four

1943

Major Cyril Arthur Joseph Martin,
ROYAL ENGINEERS

Battersea beside the Thames was the place where an unexploded bomb fell on a warehouse during the night raid of 17–18 January 1943. Vital new machinery tools delivered from America crammed the building at that particular time. This alone made the removal of the bomb crucial.

By this stage of the war, Major Martin was one of the most experienced Army officers in bomb disposal, having coped with many bombs on the capital ever since the start of the Blitz. It was natural, therefore, that Martin was asked to tackle this latest incident. He had no reason to imagine it would be any different or more difficult than the string of other cases he had undertaken and survived.

When he came to a close examination of the large bomb, however, he realized it had a brand new kind of fuse. The specific purpose of this was to make it almost impossibly dangerous to tackle by any disposal procedures then current. Martin settled on the only other approach – to attack it from the base plate and steam out the large amount of explosive that way. The theory seemed all right, anyway.

The base plate came off safely, but only to reveal solid cast TNT inside. Steam under high pressure would be the only way of extracting this. The latest procedure in such a case would be to steam out from a distance by remote control, but this could not be countenanced here, due to the danger of explosion.

Martin took the decision to go ahead by hand nozzle. In this way, he could control the flow and release only sufficient steam to soften the explosive slightly. Thereafter, scraping it free would have to be done. It proved a tedious task, not to mention the constant, terrific tension. Martin and one other Army officer were forced to lay beside the bomb in a hole choked with a combination of water and steam.

In this position, the two men went on with this steaming and scraping nonstop from mid-afternoon on 20 January until the next morning. At any time the bomb might well have exploded. Over this long period of some sixteen hours, they extracted all the TNT from the weapon. They emerged tired but triumphant and Major Martin's citation referred, almost unnecessarily, to his 'almost unbelievable and cold-blooded courage'. Martin was honorary secretary of the VC and GC Association from 1961 to 1970.

Chief Officer George Preston Stronach,
MERCHANT NAVY

George Stronach was Chief Officer of the SS *Ocean Voyager* as she lay in Tripoli harbour on 19 March 1943. Out of the Mediterranean blue sky, an enemy attack developed and she was suddenly struck by bombs and caught fire. The steamship had a large consignment of petrol and ammunition on board, which began to go off heavily and regularly. In spite of strenuous efforts by her crew to fight the flames, the ship had to be abandoned.

The initial explosion had killed the *Ocean Voyager*'s Master, so that the responsibility for further operations devolved on Stronach as second in command. The bomb-blast knocked him temporarily unconscious, but he recovered almost at once and went forward to look for survivors. He found a number of the crew sheltering in the alleyway and, ignoring the ammunition scattering in every direction, led them to a boat alongside. This plied them to safety elsewhere in the harbour.

Stronach then thought of the possibility of any further survivors, so he lowered another boat and brought it alongside the ship. The vessel was now burning furiously, but Stronach staggered almost blindly to the officers' accommodation amidships. Finding a hose with a trickle of water dribbling from it, he held this over his head to keep himself sufficiently wet for protection from the worst of both heat and flame.

Climbing into the collapsed accommodation, Stronach found one of the deck officers unconscious and badly burned. He pulled the officer clear and dragged the man's heavy frame along the deck to the boat. Returning to the accommodation, Stronach started to remove debris which was trapping another officer. Again he hauled this man through the porthole and along the deck. He then tied a rope around the man's waist and lowered him over the ship's side to the boat.

As the situation was becoming increasingly desperate, Stronach ordered the boat to be taken away to safety. Once again he returned amidships, where he disoovered yet another severely injured officer.

Dragging this man along the deck to the side of the doomed ship, Stronach tied a rope around him and lowered him over the side onto a raft, which had returned to the ship in response to his calls.

Yet again Stronach continued his search for survivors and, taking a final frantic look round aft, he saw a greaser lying unconscious in the scuppers. He got hold of the inert man and heaved him to the side of the ship. There was neither boat nor raft alongside by then, but Stronach could not delay. He slung a lifebelt around the greaser and literally threw him overboard.

When he was satisfied that there were no further survivors, the Chief Officer jumped overboard himself, actually welcoming the cool water after the furnace-like conditions aboard. He swam to a manned raft and, under his direction, they returned to pick up the injured greaser.

The *Ocean Voyager* had been likely to blow up all over Tripoli harbour at any time throughout this ordeal, yet Stronach stayed on the burning ship searching for men over what must have seemed an endless period of one hour and twenty minutes. His inspiring leadership, after the loss of the Master, enabled a number of the crew to get away to safety – while he ignored his own. He undoubtedly saved the lives of the three officers and greaser, all of whom had been badly hurt. His action equalled any in the annals of the British Merchant Navy.

Wing Commander John Samuel Rowlands,
ROYAL AIR FORCE VOLUNTEER RESERVE

Conspicuous courage in bomb disposal. One instance of this would justify recognition of some kind. Wing Commander Rowlands displayed it for two years. He made safe varied types of weapons and his total tally of individual cases ran into hundreds. Not only did he have to face fresh, and thus unknown, permutations of enemy circuitry, but there were also unexploded bombs from British and Allied aircraft. Some of these planes had crashed or made forced landings; other bombs had been released for the safety of crews in damaged aircraft.

Taking just one unusual incident as typical of Rowlands' remarkable record, a weapon in a substantial Bomber Command dump exploded. This affected many high explosive and incendiary weapons ready and prepared for offensive operations. All these weapons were damaged to some extent by the firing of the original bomb and were left in a highly unstable state. Rowlands had to contend with continuing fire, and armaments going off spasmodically. He completed this doubly daunting job successfully, just as he had done since earlier in the war. Later in life, he became an Air Marshal.

Frederick John Cradock,
BOILERMAN

On 4 May 1943, an explosion in a Suffolk boilerhouse caused it to fill with scalding steam and water. A man was trapped in a well between the furnace and the actual boiler. Frederick Cradock, in his fifty-seventh year, was in charge of the boilerhouse. At the instant of the accident, he was on top of the furnace and could easily have jumped to safety on the side distant from the steam. Instead, he refused to do so and called for a ladder. He turned into the escaping steam and tried to get down into the well to haul out his workmate.

But before he could save the man, Cradock himself was overcome by the steam and severely scalded. He staggered away from the steam and was still conscious. At this later moment, he could still have jumped to safety, but despite his injuries he returned to make a second attempt to get down into the well. He died in making this second attempt.

Leading Aircraftman Kenneth Gerald Spooner,
ROYAL CANADIAN AIR FORCE

As a student navigator in the Royal Canadian Air Force, twenty-year-old Kenneth Spooner was one of four men on a training flight near Lake Erie. It was 14 May 1943. Quite soon after the aircraft had left the runway of the Training School, their pilot fainted. Spooner could see at once that he was unlikely to regain consciousness quickly. Since none of the other navigational students would possibly pilot the machine, Spooner decided to try to do so. He assumed control of the plane and told his three fellow-trainees: 'Bale out – now.'

They all had parachutes for such an emergency and did as they were told. They pitched out in an orderly way, the parachutes deployed, and all three floated down on to Canadian soil. In the meanwhile, Spooner grappled with the aircraft controls and commeneed a landing attempt. The pilot remained unconscious. Spooner had never landed a plane, but did his best to put the aircraft in the right approach position. Unfortunately, he was not able to achieve this and the plane crashed, killing both himself and the unconscious pilot.

Private Charles Alfred Duncan,
ARMY AIR CORPS PARACHUTE REGIMENT

On 10 July 1943, Private Duncan was serving at M'Saken in North Africa when a live grenade fell amongst a group of his comrades. Realizing that it was on the point of exploding, he threw himself over it and gave his life to save theirs. Private Duncan's memorial is at the Enfidaville War Cemetery in Tunisia.

Major Andre Gilbert Kempster,
ROYAL ARMOURED CORPS

As in the case of Private Duncan, this was one of several deeds that were almost identical but by different members of the Services. The actions all concerned hand grenades. On 21 August 1943, Major Andre Kempster was in Algeria with the Duke of Wellington's Regiment of the Royal Armoured Corps. He was in a pit demonstrating grenade throwing to two of his RAC men.

Kempster tossed a grenade towards the parapet, but with tragic consequences. It failed to clear the top and bounced back towards the three men. Thinking desperately, Kempster rushed to scoop it up, but this did not prove practicable. By then, of course, the fuse time had almost expired, so Kempster unhesitatingly pitched his whole body on top of the grenade to cover its effect. When it went off, only a second or two later, there was no possibility of Kempster surviving. But in making the ultimate sacrifice, he had certainly preserved the lives of his two comrades.

Lieutenant John Bridge,
ROYAL NAVAL VOLUNTEER RESERVE

The awards of the George Cross were by now more and more reflecting the course of the war. The Allies had invaded Sicily and taken it. By August 1943, they were in Messina at the foot of Italy. The enemy had left the harbour there littered with depth charges, laid to delay and hinder the Allies in using the facilities of the port. Tackling this fresh obstacle of defensive depth charges began to cost lives. A pattern of six charges went off, resulting in the death or injury of a complete bomb disposal team.

Lieutenant John Bridge knew of this tragedy, but assumed control for the clearance of the remainder of the depth charges. It took a total of twenty-eight dives to find and dispose of those still threatening the harbour before the actual Allied landings on the Italian mainland.

Two utterly unfamiliar firing circuits were among this large batch of charges neutralized. Bridge dismantled or 'discredited' 207 more both under water and on the surface. He and his team were able to confirm that the harbour was all clear in advance of the mass Allied landings. In addition, Bridge was awarded the George Medal and Bar. He accepted the post of Assistant Education Officer, Southport, in 1947 and that of Director of Education, Sunderland, in 1963.

Captain Matreen Ahmed Ansari,
INDIAN ARMY

The British Colony of Hong Kong was taken by the Japanese in December 1941. Among the prisoners of war was Captain Ansari of the 7th Rajput Rifles, Indian Army. Ansari had close blood connections to an Indian State ruler, so the Japanese set about the task of trying to make him renege on his sympathies for Britain. They hoped that in this way Ansari might develop anti-British feeling among the other Indian prisoners. Ansari refused to comply with their hopes and so they cast him into the notorious Stanley prison the following May. Here he endured the enemy's worst treatment of brutality and food deprivation.

Later on, they moved him back to his original camp, still with Ansari insisting he would remain loyal to Britain. Just one year after his first ordeal in Stanley prison, the Japanese returned him there in May 1943. Further barbaric treatment and virtual starvation followed, finally ending with the enemy condemning him to

1. Near-miss by St Paul's Cathedral. A large time bomb at this spot fell on 17 September 1940, burying itself twenty-six feet deep. A bomb disposal unit under the command of Lieutenant R. Davies saved St Paul's by digging up the bomb and making it harmless. *(Imperial War Museum)*

2. German time bomb in the grounds of the German Hospital, London; an ironic touch. Lieutenant Davies is looking for the fuse on this 1,200-pounder. *(Imperial War Museum)*

3. German bomb-mine designed for use on land or in the water. To prevent its secrets being discovered, it was fitted with a detonating device which operated if the mine was laid in too-shallow water.

4. Leading Aircraftman Karl Gravell, Royal Canadian Air Force, made a selfless attempt to save a pilot.
(*Imperial War Museum*)

5. Malta under siege. The island suffered grievous air attacks daily for months on end.

6. Captain Dudley Mason, Merchant Navy, brought the crippled tanker *Ohio* into Malta with her crucial cargo of oil after days of relentless German air attack. *(Imperial War Museum)*

7. Sergeant Graham Parish made a heroic attempt to rescue a passenger injured in a blazing bomber. *(Imperial War Museum)*

8. Private Charles Duncan threw himself on a grenade about to explode. *(Imperial War Museum)*

9. Assistant Section Officer Noor Inayat-Khan, known by the code name 'Madeleine', was executed at Dachau in September 1944.
(Imperial War Museum)

10. Ensign Violette Szabo, Special Operations Executive, executed at Ravensbrück in January 1945.
(Imperial War Museum)

11. Albert Heming *(left)* rescued this Roman Catholic priest from a Bermondsey church hit by a bomb on 2 March 1945. *(Imperial War Museum)*

12. Wing Commander Forest Yeo-Thomas, code name 'The White Rabbit'. He was dropped into France during February 1943 and, against all the odds, survived for over two years. *(Imperial War Museum)*

13. Odette Sansom – another legendary name in Special Operations Executive. Infiltrated into France in October 1942, she was later captured, tortured and imprisoned but survived the war. *(Imperial War Museum)*

14. Flight Lieutenant John Quinton who gave up his parachute to an air cadet as his stricken Wellington bomber broke up. *(Imperial War Museum)*

15. HM The Queen presenting the George Cross to the Royal Ulster Constabulary. It was accepted on behalf of the entire RUC by Constable Paul Slaine who had lost both his legs in an attack by Provisional IRA terrorists in 1992.

16. Eighteen-year-old Trooper Christopher Finney was awarded the George Cross for his heroism in Iraq on 28 March 2003. Although injured as a result of a 'friendly fire' air attack, he rescued a comrade from a burning armoured vehicle and gallantly attempted to save another.

death. In October 1943, Captain Ansari was executed, together with thirty other Indian, British and Chinese prisoners of war. His George Cross award stressed how his behaviour had made it easier for other prisoners not to subvert. The date of his death was 29 October 1943 and he is commemorated in the Stanley Military Cemetery, Hong Kong.

John Alexander Fraser

Pearl Harbor marked the start of the Far East war. John Fraser was then Assistant Attorney-General in the Colonial Service and was attached to the British Army Aid Group.

Along with many others, Fraser was interned in the Civilian Internment Camp at Stanley. Wasting hardly any time, he started to organize escape plans and also a secret wireless service for the prisoners. Fraser was aware of the fearful risks that he ran, but he went on with all his activities, successfully getting news from the outside world and passing important information out of the camp.

Eventually the inevitable happened. He was arrested and subjected to long bouts of severe torture by the Japanese. The enemy were determined to extract information from him and force him to implicate others who were working with him. Under this inhuman treatment, he never uttered one word that would help the investigations of his persecutors or bring possible punishment to other prisoners.

The incredible fortitude of this Scotsman was such that even the Japanese guards commented on his courage. Fraser inspired other prisoners and certainly saved the lives of his helpers. The enemy were unable to break his spirit and finally executed him on 29 October 1943. Fraser won the Military Cross and Bar in the First World War. Three years to the day after he died, on 29 October 1946, the George Cross was added posthumously to his other honours.

Sergeant John Rennie,
THE ARGYLL AND SUTHERLAND HIGHLANDERS OF CANADA

Another accident involving grenades. On 29 October 1943, the Canadians were in Britain in large numbers to prepare for D-Day and the final assault on Germany. A unit was engaged in the exercise of throwing grenades. The location was a Canadian Training Camp near Slough in Buckinghamshire. One of these small but deadly weapons did not carry clear of the embankment above the men under training but started to return down the slope towards the Canadian soldiers.

Sergeant Rennie estimated its path, ran in a direction to intercept it and attempted to hurl it clear. But tragically, the fuse time had elapsed and the grenade shattered the surrounding area. It killed Rennie, but by his heroism he had broken the blast between the fragmenting grenade and three of the troops, standing less than half-a-dozen paces from the spot.

Private Joseph Henry Silk,
SOMERSET LIGHT INFANTRY

The fighting forces had more than enough to face throughout Second World War, without the inevitability of occasional tragic mishaps. This one occurred in Burma on 4 December 1943 in the theatre sometimes described as 'the forgotten war'.

Private Silk and others in his platoon of the Somerset Light Infantry were busy cleaning various weapons on sloping jungle territory. Some of Silk's platoon were close by, while higher and lower on the slope, other troops were also engaged in the same duties.

Suddenly one of Silk's grenades started to fizz alight and then to hiss. He thought in what must have been a mere nano-second. Calling loudly for anyone within earshot to take cover, he fell on the grenade, pressed it to his body, and shielded the men near him as much as he could. When it went off a few seconds afterwards, Silk was killed and two of his comrades hurt a little. Silk knew there were infantry all around him in grenade range and decided on his own death instead of the chance of theirs.

Meanwhile, the forgotten war went on, oblivious to this gesture from one twenty-seven-year-old private of the Somerset Light Infantry. His memorial is in Rangoon and he is not forgotten.

Captain Douglas Ford,
THE ROYAL SCOTS
Colonel Lanceray Arthur Newnham,
THE MIDDLESEX REGIMENT

Along with many other Britons, Captain Ford of The Royal Scots fell into Japanese hands in Hong Kong when the Colony was invaded. Colonel Newnham was captured at the same time – in December 1941. Together with some other British prisoners, Ford and Newnham managed to make contact with British agents during the following year. The idea was to plan for a large-scale breakout from the camp but, unfortunately, written matter between prisoners and agents was intercepted by the enemy and the escape organization was discovered.

Ford and Newnham endured arrest, questioning, starvation and torture. This began on 10 July 1943 until they received a summary sentence of death to try to force them to disclose the names of others in the breakout plan. They resisted to the end, however, and both officers were executed at Sham Shui Po Prisoner Camp on the same day – 18 December 1943. With many others, they are both commemorated for their courage at the Stanley Military Cemetery, Hong Kong.

Flight Lieutenant Hector Bertram Gray,
ROYAL AIR FORCE

Along with Captain Ford and Colonel Newnham, Flight Lieutenant Gray was another British officer taken prisoner at the fall of Hong Kong. Gray smuggled medical supplies into their camp which were crucial for the many seriously sick prisoners. In addition, he circulated news from outside to help keep up morale. Gray was subjected to the usual unspeakable torture by his captors to try to extract names of his helpers. Gray died in the same manner as Ford and Newnham – and on the same day, one week before Christmas.

Chapter Five

1944

Captain Jenkin Robert Oswald Thompson,
ROYAL ARMY MEDICAL CORPS

It was now 1944. But the unique aspect of the award made in the name of Captain Thompson was that it quoted his gallantry during four separate major episodes of the war when he was serving in the Royal Army Medical Corps aboard hospital carrier ships.

The first was in late May 1940 at Dunkirk aboard the *Paris*. The second on 10–14 July 1943 during the Sicily landings aboard the *St David*. The third was on 10–15 September 1943 at Salerno, Italy, also on the *St David*, and the fourth on 23–24 January at Anzio, again aboard the *St David*. Each time during these four epic actions, Thompson ignored dive-bombing and shells from enemy guns and tended to his patients throughout hours and days of danger.

Then over the night of 24 January 1944, during the fury of the attack at Anzio, HM Hospital Carrier *St David* sustained a hit by dive-bomber. As a result of this intentional strike, the long-serving mercy ship began to sink. From his long experience in maritime emergencies, Thompson saw that the most severely wounded of the patients in his care were borne into lifeboats safely. Through his calmness and courage in a nightmare background all but one patient from his own ward were saved – together with less serious cases from some other wards. The carrier clearly had only the briefest time left afloat.

'Abandon Ship.'

'Every man for himself.'

On these commands, Thompson went below yet again to try to save the sole patient remaining. Despite a superhuman struggle to do so, he could not move this man. Thompson stayed with him to the end.

Brigadier Arthur Frederick Crane Nicholls,
COLDSTREAM GUARDS

Albania was the remote and rather unlikely destination of Brigadier Nicholls as he checked his parachute before jumping in October 1943. Nicholls' title was General Staff Officer to the Allied Military Mission. The purpose of this organization was developing local resistance in enemy-occupied Albania. Unfortunately, the Germans made an assault on the Mission, who had to break up urgently.

Over the midwinter months until January 1944, Nicholls was on the run amid icy weather and harsh mountain terrain. Frostbite attacked him so drastically that he had no choice but to authorize someone without due experience to cut off both his legs, with no anaesthetic. Two men hauled him across the hostile mountains, while Nicholls was lying on his winter coat.

Nicholls had the closest British Mission as his goal and, by astounding willpower, kept going until he got there. Future Allied actions depended on his assessments in the report he made. Once having achieved his aim, Brigadier Nicholls could not fight his physical condition any longer. Heart failure and gangrene caused his death on 11 February 1944.

Leslie Owen Fox,
LONDON COUNTY COUNCIL HEAVY RESCUE SERVICE

By 20 February 1944, raids had returned to London. Bombs had demolished a house in Fulham, West London. The wreckage was on fire and the remaining walls were in a critical condition liable to collapse. The entire framework was well alight.

At this stage, cries were heard from under part of the rubble. Leslie Fox, a deputy rescue party leader, began to tunnel his way through the ruins. Masonry and other matter passed back by Fox was frequently too hot to be held, and his men continually sprayed him with water in an endeavour to keep down the almost intolerable heat.

At great personal danger, Fox shored up the entrance to his tunnel, which ran alongside an unstable party wall. After about two hours of very strenuous struggle, Fox found the casualty. By then, Fox was in a distressed state, but he refused to allow a relief to take his place and he continued to operate.

Then the dangerous wall did indeed collapse, blocking the tunnel entrance and causing the structure to subside. Yet Fox recommenced tunnelling. Two further hours and he was once more in a condition approaching physical collapse. By sheer personal perseverance, he had tunnelled fifteen feet and cleared the debris away from the head of the trapped man whose feet were still under a mound of rubble. Fox also managed to cover him with some sort of protection.

A medical officer then got through to the casualty and administered much-needed restoratives. The man was eventually brought back to safety, from almost certain death. This was due to the tenacity of Leslie Fox and his rescue team.

Richard Arthur Samuel Bywater,
FACTORY DEVELOPMENT OFFICER

Three-and-a-half months before D-Day, all the many Royal Ordnance Factories were working at double pressure to manufacture the stockpile of munitions needed for the Normandy invasion. Many of these and other factories on war work were scattered throughout the North of England and the Midlands. One of these ROFs, attached to the Ministry of Supply, was at Kirkby, near Liverpool. No fewer than 10,000 staff were manufacturing a variety of munitions, including a weekly total of 150,000 anti-tank mine fuses. These had the dual characteristics of a sensitive mechanism and highly powerful charge.

It was the morning of 22 February 1944 and nineteen operators, most of them women, were working on a late stage of filling fuses. Each operative had a tray of twenty-five fuses on a bench, while around them were other trays on portable tables. Each table held a stack of forty trays, so that one operative had about 1,000 fuses either filled with explosive or waiting to be filled. There were some 12,000 fuses in the factory building at that moment.

It was between 8.20 a.m. and 8.30 a.m. in the morning. One of the fuses suddenly exploded, at once detonating its whole tray of twenty-four. The girl working on the particular bench was blown up instantly, while the others behind her received injuries – one of them fatal. The building itself was badly damaged, with its roof torn off. The factory's electrical equipment was left dangling in mid-air.

The superintendent of the factory arrived within a minute or two, with Arthur Bywater, the development officer. They realized that it would not take much to set off all the several thousands of filled fuses, with consequent massive material havoc and loss of life. Bywater took over control of the situation, rapidly organizing the orderly evacuation of this and all adjacent buildings. He next led a team of three volunteers to look at the fuses, get rid of any damaged or defective ones and move the rest to a safe place.

The explanation for the original explosion seemed to have been a defective striker, which could, of course, be present in some of the other fuses. So it was a hazardous job. Bywater inspired the other three helpers to work on day and night. By 5 p.m. on the second day, 4,000 fuses with defective strikers had not only been identified but shifted to a burning ground a mile or so distant. Apart from these fuses, the team went on for nearly seventy-two hours altogether removing 12,724 fuses from the shattered factory.

Among the 4,000 defective fuses, Bywater categorized twenty-three as critically sensitive. He bore each one of these out of the factory and destroyed it with a controlled explosion.

One fuse had reached such a state of sensitivity that Bywater recognized it could and would go off with the merest shudder or vibration. He tiptoed out of the factory with it, thrust it into a safe, and set it off with a guncotton charge. The chances of Bywater surviving those three days and nights were regarded as minimal by explosives experts, but he did.

The sequel to the story came seven months later, when an even more serious explosive accident happened, also at the Kirkby factory. Now it was the autumn of 1944 and once again Arthur Bywater showed the same qualities of leadership and courage. For the first accident, he received the George Cross. For his heroism on this second occasion, he won the George Medal. He was the only civilian to have been awarded both the George Cross and George Medal. He died in 2005, at the age of ninety-one.

Anthony Smith,
CIVIL DEFENCE RESCUE SERVICE

Anthony Smith was a chimney sweep in London and also a member of the Civil Defence Rescue Service. During an air raid on 25 February 1944, a stick of bombs fell at World's End, Chelsea, demolishing a four-storey building. Only the party walls remained and these only precariously so. Gas and water mains had been fractured and gas actually ignited, setting fire to both building and wreckage.

An eyewitness described the scene as 'a raging inferno'.

Two floors had pancaked, forming a huge pile of blazing debris, but Anthony Smith decided to burrow a way through this and managed to reach a casualty trapped in a front basement. He released the victim, but by that time the front of the building presented a solid sheet of flame, the upper floors were crumbling inwards and his escape route had been cut off.

Carrying the casualty, Smith forced a way through the smoke and fire to reach the rear of the house. He found a six-inch aperture amid the wreckage. Somehow he burrowed away to enlarge a way through it and to pass the casualty to safety just as the remaining portion of the front wall collapsed.

The heat and general conditions burnt Smith's eyebrows and hair and he was all but overcome by the actual smoke. In those days, it was not always realized how lethal smoke could be. Undeterred by all this, though, he went to the assistance of a comrade in the rescue service who was trying to reach a woman trapped in the basement of an adjoining building. The walls here were also in a highly dangerous state.

Smith worked for an hour up to his waist in water and with walls and floors all on the point of disintegrating. He was able to help in the rescue and release of the woman and then carried on until his squad was duly relieved of their duties.

Subedar Subramanian

24 February 1944: as the Allies slogged their tortuous way up Italy, they reached Mignano. Subramanian was a subedar in the Queen Victoria's Own Madras Sappers and Miners. Out of the blue, he realized that a mine was about to explode. In a semi-second he spreadeagled himself over it as it erupted. Through his action none of the sappers and miners was hurt. Subramanian lay dead.

Captain Lionel Colin Matthews,
AUSTRALIAN MILITARY FORCES

A captain in the Corps of Signals, Australian Military Forces, Lionel Matthews hailed from South Australia and had won the Military Cross before the fall of Singapore on 15 February 1942. Matthews was among the thousands of Allied troops taken by the Japanese on that fateful date.

It would be too painful to chronicle his suffering throughout the ensuing two years. He was barbarically treated and tortured to try to force intelligence from him that would have betrayed fellow prisoners and helped the enemy. It was an interminable time, but Matthews neither talked nor helped. In the end, the Japanese took the ultimate step and executed him on 2 March 1944 at Kuching in Borneo. He and all the others like him should never be forgotten. Nor are they. Decades later, places like Changi on Singapore still resonate with the memory of the men who died there – and elsewhere.

Benjamin Gimbert,
DRIVER, LONDON NORTH EASTERN RAILWAY
James William Nightall,
FIREMAN, LONDON NORTH EASTERN RAILWAY

On 2 June 1944, just ninety-six hours before the D-Day landings, an ammunition train of fifty-one trucks was pulling into Soham station in Cambridgeshire. The trucks were filled with unfused bombs bound for US Air Force bases throughout East Anglia. The consignment could hardly have been more vital.

Benjamin Gimbert, driving the train, suddenly discovered that the goods wagon next to his engine was on fire. This wagon was carrying forty 500-pound bombs. Gimbert immediately drew the attention of the fireman, James Nightall, to the emergency as he started to bring the train to a standstill. At the same time, Gimbert alerted the guard and signalman by blasts on the whistle of the train.

By the time the train had stopped, flames enveloped the whole of the truck. Appreciating the dire danger this posed to the entire train of fifty other trucks, Gimbert instructed Nightall to try to uncouple the truck behind the blazing one. Nightall knew that both trucks contained explosives, but leapt down from the foot-plate and began to uncouple the trucks with a hammer. Then he ran forward again and rejoined Gimbert.

So the rest of the train was now separated from the blazing van. This still stood close to the station buildings and remained a potential threat that could endanger life in the village of Soham. They decided they had to get the burning truck further away from the remainder of the wagons and run it into the open.

Gimbert set his engine in motion and as he approached a signal box he warned the signalman to stop any other trains which were likely to be involved, indicating by hand what he intended to do. The mail train would shortly be due on the opposite line.

Almost at that second, the bombs on the burning van blew up. The fireman, James Nightall, was killed and Gimbert very severely injured. The crater measured twenty feet deep and sixty feet across. This was formed in the railway track itself. This explosion destroyed or damaged many buildings, including the Soham station and nearby structures. The engine of the ammunition train toppled on its side. Beneath it lay James Nightall, while the signalman perished later from his injuries. The eruption blew Benjamin sky high, but did not kill him. Over thirty metal fragments lodged in his body, to be removed later.

Both Gimbert and Nightall knew the lethal nature of the train, and especially of the wagon on fire. They showed courage and resourcefulness in trying to isolate it. They could, with justification, have left the train and sought shelter, but chose to risk their lives to protect the other fifty wagons. Not only did they prevent the rest of the train from exploding, they saved its precious ammunition at a critical moment for the Allies immediately before D-Day. Gimbert has various commemorations in Soham and he had a locomotive honouring his name.

Lieutenant Leon Verdi Goldsworthy,
ROYAL AUSTRALIAN NAVAL VOLUNTEER RESERVE

The third in the trio of Australian naval officers in Enemy Mining Section, HMS *Vernon* was Lieutenant Goldsworthy, from Broken Hill, New South Wales. Goldsworthy specialized in recovering mines and actually rendering them safe while under water. He made a series of such recoveries over the crucial ten-month period from June 1943 to April 1944. Enemy ground mines, magnetic mines and an acoustic mine were among his 'bag'.

But these successes occurred against an occasional tragedy like the one at Falmouth in Cornwall. A Dornier dropped five bombs on the town one Saturday afternoon in the spring, and then laid a mine on the return run. This had to be rendered safe. The Royal Navy had three divers with some experience: Sub Lieutenant R.B. Sutherland and Divers Tawn and Wharton.

Sub Lieutenant Sutherland had found the mine originally and now re-located it in three fathoms only a furlong from the Custom House Quay. It was believed to be magnetic, but could have been an acoustic. Sutherland had the support of Tawn and Wharton in charge of the telephone and guide rope on the diving boat above. They were in company with a minimum crew of three other naval ratings.

On the second dive of the day, Sutherland said in a thin metallic voice over the phone: 'O.K. I'm on the bottom.'

He knew that the mine could still be live. If it was an acoustic weapon, the slightest sound could kill him. As he groped forward to put a cap-fitting over the fuse, a slight sound must have been inevitable; a faint, low-pitched note on the bed of the harbour. Nothing more. One note. The microphone or vibrator in the mine responded to it; a minute current surged through the circuit, a switch was made, primer and detonator fired . . . and a column of water fountained up 200 feet high.

Six precious lives were lost, including the three valuable divers.

After the affair at Falmouth, the need became apparent and urgent for a self-contained diving suit to undertake such search and recovery operations. Armitage and Mould developed a suit, and to counter any possible effect it might produce on a magnetic mine, only non-magnetic metal was used for parts like the helmet.

Goldsworthy played a prominent role in the trials of this suit, which proved itself repeatedly in subsequent underwater operations. It was Goldsworthy who, in April 1944 found himself diving after an acoustic specimen in Milford Haven harbour. Everything was going to plan. He pulled on his guide rope to signify that he wanted to surface. Slowly he was hauled up.

A fair swell was running – it was around the time of the spring tides – and the little launch lurched and rolled with the water, tugging fretfully at her anchor. Goldsworthy was a small man but as strong as any in that tough trio of Aussies on enemy mine work. He fell foul of the ladder under the boat. He lost his footing, groped for a moment, and hit his helmet against the hull. He hung there suspended. A joint came loose. The water poured in. He spluttered. Bubbles from his air-supply shot up to the surface only a few feet above.

His attendant took one look at the first stream of them, plunged overboard, grabbed him quickly, and hauled him clear of the ladder. The rest of the crew got him inboard. The choking mist cleared as Goldsworthy lay in the bottom of the boat. He opened his eyes. 'Thanks, cobber,' he croaked. A narrow squeak. All the damage he suffered was a jarred spine.

June 1944. D-Day came and went. Both Britain and Germany had developed 'oyster' mines, operated by pressure from a ship on the water between it and the mine on the bottom. Only one German specimen had been found so far, at Luc-sur-Mer, so Goldsworthy was sent over to Seine Bay to try to capture under water any new ground mines and an 'oyster'. Wherever they were, he had to dive for them.

The beachheads had been secured, certainly, but shells still dropped in the waters of the bay; mines were being swept and blown up all along the coast and the Allies fired depth charges regularly to keep U-boats at bay. Goldsworthy went down amid all these explosions, knowing that if any of them occurred within a mile of him, he would be liable to feel a fatal effect through the water. He went down again and again. Through the sea throbbed the sounds of war, from far and near. He was a sitting target. A stray mine did explode 2,000 yards off. It jolted him as he searched at six fathoms. But nothing nearer. Goldy lived. He did not find an 'oyster' – but he lived to dive another day. That was the main thing. In fact, all three Royal Australian Naval Volunteer Reserve officers of Enemy Mining Section survived the war.

Air Commodore Arthur Dwight Ross,
ROYAL CANADIAN AIR FORCE

On the last day of June 1944, an accident occurred at RAF Tholthorpe in Yorkshire. During a night landing, a Halifax returning from an operation collided with another bomber. This second aircraft had been about to take off. The impact was so severe that the Halifax split into three parts and caught fire.

Air Commodore Ross was awaiting the operational crews' return for the usual debriefing. As soon as he saw the crash, he and a corporal rushed to the scene. Ross managed to save the severely hurt pilot just as a large fused bomb in the other aircraft was triggered by the collision. Although the other bomber stood some eighty yards distant from them, the blast hurled both men to the tarmac.

As the dust and debris settled, they heard calls for help from the rear turret of the broken Halifax. Flaming bombs and fuel were causing double danger for the Air Commodore and Corporal, but they both forced their way to the wrecked turret to try to get at the trapped rear gunner who had shouted for help. Ross axed desperately at the perspex, now burning and melting. Behind the perspex, the rear gunner was still alive. At that stage another bomb burst and all but severed the Air Commodore's arm. Somehow they rescued the rear gunner, while Ross actually walked to a waiting ambulance under his own power. There was no time to delay treatment to Ross's deteriorating condition, so at the RAF sick quarters the staff carried out an immediate emergency operation to amputate the shattered arm. After the war his last appointment was commanding the 5th Canadian Air Force, before his retirement in 1959.

Sowar Ditto Ram,
CENTRAL INDIA HORSE (21ST KING GEORGE V'S OWN HORSE),
INDIAN ARMOURED CORPS

In Normandy the Allies were advancing. In Italy two men won the George Cross on the same night and at the same place. Sowar Ditto Ram was a member of a patrol ordered to occupy a hill. On reaching the objective, the patrol ran on to an enemy minefield. They suffered serious casualties to five men, including Ditto Ram. In fact his injuries must have ranked as some of the worst, as a mine blew off his left leg below the knee.

Ditto Sam actually applied a field dressing in the darkness. Then he heard muted calls for help from another Sowar who had been wounded, so he crawled forward through the minefield to help or at least comfort the man. Ditto Ram was all too aware of the damage that the mines could inflict.

When he reached the other Sowar, he found that the man's left thigh had been shattered. Ditto Ram somehow stayed conscious in spite of the loss of his own leg, and put a field dressing on his comrade's wound. This proved a protracted and complicated job, yet he forced himself to remain conscious until it was completed. Only a few minutes later, Ditto Ram died.

Sowar Ditto Ram was a very young soldier with two years' service, yet he behaved in the manner of the most mature man in his Corps. And he died without a murmur of complaint. No one will ever know whether he acted primarily for his own country, the Allies, his comrade, or his deepest self. Perhaps this unanswered question applied to many others who made such sacrifices.

Lieutenant St John Graham Young,
ROYAL TANK REGIMENT

23–24 July 1944: the same night and the same place. Both Ditto Ram and Lieutenant Young had the George Cross bestowed through almost identically superhuman efforts.

Young was in charge of a night patrol by the Central India Horse when they found themselves in the middle of a minefield. The Royal Tank Regiment lieutenant, attached to the Indian Armoured Corps, later crawled on hands and knees towards one of his men who had set off a mine and been badly hurt. On his way, Young rendered safe three of these mines before kneeling on another one. Its explosion severed the officer's right leg, yet he crawled on forward to reach the injured soldier and apply a dressing.

For the next five hours, until the Italian dawn, Young went on exhorting his men before being reached and carried to safety. Young became unconscious soon afterwards and although surviving throughout the rest of 24 July, he died during the evening. So the twenty-three-year-old Lieutenant made the same sacrifice as the still-younger Sowar Ditto Ram.

Private Benjamin Gower Hardy
22ND AUSTRALIAN GARRISON, AUSTRALIAN MILITARY FORCES
Private Ralph Jones
22ND AUSTRALIAN GARRISON, AUSTRALIAN MILITARY FORCES

It was 2 a.m. in Australia on the night of 4–5 August 1944. Privates Hardy and Jones were on duty at No. 12 Prisoner of War Camp, Cowra, New South Wales, as members of a machine-gun crew. They were guarding the compound which housed over 1,100 Japanese internees.

Unknown to Hardy and Jones, and the rest of the Australians guarding the camp, the Japanese planned a major breakout attempt at 2 a.m.. Armed with knives, baseball bats and other weapons, they stormed out of their huts, having first set them on fire. Aiming for the perimeter wire of the camp, they bore down en masse on the machine-gun crew. Hardy and Jones, both in their mid-forties, stood their ground in the face of this terrifying onslaught from 1,000 of the enemy. The two Australian soldiers continued to work their gun until they were overrun and 'bashed to death'.

The end of the story was this: Hardy and Jones had won a little time for the other Australian guards, who swung into action and hit many of the enemy with fire from another machine gun. Most of the remainder surrendered at dawn, or were caught later, or committed suicide. The two George Cross awards to Hardy and Jones were, of course, posthumous.

Corporal Kenneth Horsfield,
THE MANCHESTER REGIMENT, ATTACHED TO THE SPECIAL AIR SERVICE

While attached to the Special Air Service, Corporal Horsfield was working in a demolition region at Bari, southern Italy, on 18

August 1944. Suddenly, ammunition went off by accident, entrapping one of Horsfield's colleagues under a rain of rubble. At once, Horsfield tried to rescue the man, amid danger of further detonations. While still making these efforts on the man's behalf, another large blast shook the area inflicting multiple wounds on Horsfield. He was rushed from Bari to Brindisi, but his injuries proved too deep-rooted and he died.

Flying Officer Roderick Borden Gray,
ROYAL CANADIAN AIR FORCE

The desolate setting was the Atlantic Ocean on the night of 27 August 1944. An enemy U-boat shot down a Wellington bomber, which crash-landed in the sea. The navigator of the aircraft, Roderick Gray, managed to extricate himself, together with three other members of the crew. Gray sustained a severe leg wound, but succeeded in inflating his own dinghy and then helped the Wellington's captain into it. Like Gray, the captain had also been wounded in the crash landing.

Shortly afterwards, they heard cries out of the gloom from another of the aircrew, who had broken his arm and was obviously in distress. Gray also helped him into the dinghy. Gray knew that the dinghy could only hold two men, and refused to get into the slight sanctuary of the dinghy.

By then, Gray was in intense pain. Aided by another member of the crew and by an occupant of the dinghy, Gray held on to its side for some hours. All the while, the pain from his leg was intensifying and he was becoming more exhausted. It was probable that the lower part of his leg had actually been shot off. Through all this, Gray steadfastly refused to endanger the other crew by boarding the dinghy. In the end, the inevitable happened; he lost consciousness and died. When daylight eventually edged over the water from Europe, the others realized that Gray had not survived and were forced to let his body sink. The rest were rescued later and recounted the last hours of Roderick Gray, Flying Officer of the Royal Canadian Air Force.

Assistant Section Officer Noor Inayat-Khan,
WOMEN'S AUXILIARY AIR FORCE, SECONDED TO WOMEN'S TRANSPORT SERVICE (FANY)

Madeleine was the code name of Noor Inayat-Khan. The immortal Madeleine was landed in France on 16 June 1943 by Lysander.

During the weeks immediately after this, the Gestapo made mass arrests in the Paris Resistance groups to which Inayat-Khan had been assigned. This posting had become the principal and most dangerous one in France, and although given the choice to return to England, she refused to abandon it. If she had done so, she knew she would have left her French comrades without communications at a critical time. She hoped to rebuild the group after the disastrous period of the arrests. Inayat-Khan was a trained wireless operator, so strove to maintain the link with London. At that stage, she was in fact the sole contact with the capital.

The Grestapo had a full description of her, but knew only her code name. They mustered powerful forces to try to catch her and so snap this last link. She continued for a further three-and-a-half months, but then was betrayed for about seventy-five francs. The Gestapo took her to their headquarters in Avenue Foch. They had found her codes and messages, so were then in a position to work back to London.

They asked her to cooperate but she refused and gave them no further information of any kind. Inayat-Khan was imprisoned in one of the cells on the fifth floor at Avenue Foch and kept there for several weeks. She actually made two attempts to escape. She was then asked to sign a declaration that she would not make any more attempts, but she refused. The chief of the Gestapo got permission from Berlin to send her to Germany for 'safe custody' and she became the first agent to go there.

Noor Inayat-Khan reached Karlsruhe in November 1943 and again resisted the Gestapo when interrogated for further information about her work or her colleagues. From Karlsruhe they dispatched her to Pforzheim, where her cell was apart from the main prison. The director of the prison considered her to be particularly dangerous and uncooperative.

After surviving for ten months at Pforzheim, she was suddenly summoned and escorted to a railway station, where she met two other British women agents. They did not know it, but their journey would be brief. Their destination was Dachau.

There on the morning of 13 September 1944, the three girls were led out of their cells and shot through the back of the head. Their bodies were immediately cremated. For her moral and physical courage over a period exceeding a year, Noor Inayat-Khan was posthumously awarded the George Cross and the Croix de Guerre.

Major Hugh Paul Seagrim,
19TH HYDERABAD REGIMENT, ATTACHED TO FORCE 136

Burma was the setting for many heartrending stories of non-combatant gallantry. Hampshire-born Major Seagrim was in command of a special group fighting in the Karen Hills of Burma for a year from February 1943 to 1944. Seagrim was one of the four officers in this special force, two of them being British and one a Karen.

They operated successfully until late in 1943, when the enemy became aware of the existence of such a group. The Japanese launched a merciless scheme involving torture to try to locate and intercept them. Sooner or later it was inevitable that such a blanket campaign would yield results and, in February 1944, it did. They laid an ambush for the force. Seagrim's two fellow-British officers were killed and the Major and Karen officer dissolved into the temporary invisibility of the Burmese jungle.

The Japanese were so furious that only two of their four targets had been caught and killed that no fewer than 270 local Karens were rounded up. Some of these were elders and headmen, but irrespective of that, the enemy began systematically torturing and slaughtering them. At this critical stage, the Karens continued to keep Seagrim's exact whereabouts hidden. The Major was in constant touch with the atrocities in progress and felt he could not contemplate any more on his behalf. Major Seagrim surrendered on 15 March 1944.

The Japanese moved him to Rangoon, in company with eight other men and condemned them to death. Seagrim tried to reason with the enemy and plead for the other prisoners. He begged the Japanese to execute only him, since the others had only been carrying out his specific commands. The inspiring yet horrifying denouement came in September 1944. The Karens insisted that they were to suffer the same sentence as Seagrim himself, and the Japanese executed all nine men. It was one of their many atrocities in the Second World War. Major Seagrim had already won the Distinguished Service Order and the MBE. To these were added the posthumous award of the George Cross. His brother Lieutenant D.A. Seagrim, was awarded the Victoria Cross posthumously for valour in North Africa.

Sergeant Arthur Banks,
112 SQUADRON, DESERT AIR FORCE, ROYAL AIR FORCE VOLUNTEER RESERVE

In late-August 1944, Sergeant Banks, a Welshman, was one of the aircrew of an RAF aircraft taking part in an armed reconnaissance of the Ravenna and Ferrara areas of Italy. During the sortie, enemy anti-aircraft fire damaged the plane, which was compelled to make a forced landing.

After the aircraft had been destroyed, Sergeant Banks decided to try to reach the Allied lines. He managed to make contact with a group of Italian partisans quite quickly and became an outstanding figure among them. He spent the following three months advising and encouraging them in their plans and actions against the enemy.

Early in December, they mounted an attempt to cross into Allied-held territory by boat. Banks and a number of partisans assembled at their allotted place, but the enemy must have got prior knowledge of the plan, and the whole party was surrounded and captured.

Sergeant Banks was handed over to the German commander of the particular Italian district, who presided at his interrogation. During this questioning, his captors tortured him cruelly to try to extract information about the partisans. At one stage, he succeeded somehow in grabbing a light machine gun from one of the Germans. He might even have killed most of his captors, but one of the partisans intervened and pinned his arms to his sides. The man was obviously fearful of even worse treatment from the Germans. Subsequently Banks was knocked about badly before being put in prison.

Then on 8 December, Banks and a number of partisans were taken to a prison at Adria. There they stayed until 19 December, when Banks was handed over to the commander of a detachment of the Black Brigade. He was transferred to yet another prison, at Ariano Polesine.

Here, in the presence of Italian fascists, he was stripped of his clothing and again tortured. Banks still refused to divulge anything. Eventually the enemy bound him and threw him into the River Po. Despite his wounds, even then he struggled to swim or reach the river bank. The fascists caught him, took him back to the prison and he was shot through the head. He was known to have been a member of the Royal Air Force Volunteer Reserve, so the treatment he received and his ultimate fate was in direct contravention of the Geneva Convention for prisoners of war. Sergeant Banks died on 20 December 1944.

Captain Simmon Latutin,
SOMERSET LIGHT INFANTRY

Although Captain Latutin was an officer of the Somerset Light Infantry, he was seconded to the Somalia Gendarmerie. He was serving in Mogadishu, where a fire broke out in the training school on 29 December 1944. The rocket store was the seat of the conflagration. At the time, Latutin was in this store with three others – an officer, the company sergeant major and a boy. They were selecting explosives at the time when the rockets started firing.

Latutin's fellow officer became burned and virtually lost consciousness, but Latutin somehow hauled him clear of the store. Although he himself was actually alight, the Captain went back into the inferno and succeeded in saving the company sergeant major. Sadly, the boy was lost in the fire. Captain Latutin received prompt treatment for the injuries inflicted, but he had been too badly burned and died on the following day, 30 December 1944.

So into the last year of the Second World War . . .

Chapter Six

1945

Signalman Kenneth Smith,
ROYAL CORPS OF SIGNALS

The island of Ist in the Adriatic was the unique, if tragic, setting for the George Cross award made to Signalman Kenneth Smith. Working for the Royal Corps of Signals on this remote island, Smith was billeted with members of his military detachment, as well as some civilian partisans and children.

The Army expected and encountered sabotage against them almost every day, so 10 January 1945 seemed little different from any other at the time. But a time bomb was discovered by Smith in the house where this mixture of military and partisans lived. Worse than this, he heard it already ticking. Smith acted on impulse; he managed to convey it out of the house as fast as he could but just as he got clear it blew up, killing him instantly. Smith's memorial is in the Belgrade War Cemetery.

Sergeant Eric George Bailey,
NEW SOUTH WALES POLICE

Summertime in Australia. On the evening of 12 January 1945, Constable 1st Class Eric Bailey was on duty in Adelaide Street, Blayney. At about 8.30 p.m., he had occasion to stop and speak to a man whose movements seemed suspicious to him.

Soon after the Constable started to question the suspect, the man suddenly pulled a revolver from one of his pockets and fired a shot. Bailey was struck in the stomach. The policeman ignored this injury and closed with his assailant, who fired two more shots. Bailey was succumbing fast to his injuries and suffering from the joint effects of shock and haemorrhage, but he continued to struggle with the offender and actually held him on the ground until assistance appeared.

Bailey died only minutes later. He had shown great fortitude in spite of his gunshot wounds. So even in wartime, men not actively serving in armed forces equalled their counterparts in risking lives to fight against the forces of evil.

Ensign Violette Reine Elizabeth Szabo,
WOMEN'S TRANSPORT SERVICE (FANY)

After Noor Inayat-Khan, Violette Szabo was perhaps the most legendary woman of the SOE to earn the George Cross. And like Noor, Violette suffered a similar destiny. Violette was twenty-two when dropped into France in April 1944, less than two months before D-Day. She was on a highly risky operation at an especially vulnerable time. Her job was to serve as courier for a French Resistance leader whose group, based in Rouen, had been shattered.

Rouen was a geographically crucial region in 1944 and the group leader was aiming to reform his contacts and links for future action. Violette had the nerve-racking role of actually travelling between Rouen and Paris, at the same time avoiding arousing any suspicion by her movements. Her leader was at the Paris end, and Violette reported to him details of probable Resistance members still free from surveillance. She carried out this job without blemish, in fact so well that she was summoned back to England before D-Day.

But this was not the end of Violette Szabo's story. As soon as D+2 – 8 June 1944 – she found herself back on French soil with further orders to help the Resistance. This time, however, Violette was less lucky. While moving across country with her young Frenchman guide, an enemy patrol ambushed the pair. Violette was wounded, though the Frenchman was not. She knew she could not escape capture, but she made the Frenchman do so to continue their work.

It was a desperate predicament. The Germans escorted her to Limoges and then to Paris. They treated her brutally throughout the following weeks, but extracted no intelligence from her. In transit by train to Germany, an Allied air raid developed and her captors left her to scamper for shelter. At this stage, Violette was chained by the ankle to a second prisoner. Somehow, though, she got water to wounded British officers, who were able to tell their story later. Violette was incarcerated first at the notorious camp of Ravensbrück, followed by time in two labour camps. It is hardly necessary, and too painful, to record the details of conditions at these forced-labour camps. Violette was sent back to Ravensbrück early in 1945, where the Germans executed her a few months before their final surrender. So died Violette Szabo, second heroine of the SOE.

Flight Sergeant Stanley James Woodbridge,
ROYAL AIR FORCE VOLUNTEER RESERVE

Down in the jungles of Burma, the Allies were still slogging on against the Japanese. On 31 January 1945, a Liberator bomber flew over the combatants while engaged in a special operation. Tragically, the bomber crash-landed in the jungle, presumably because of being hit from the ground.

Along with five other members of the aircrew, the wireless operator, Stanley Woodbridge, was captured by the enemy. Contrary to all conventions of war, the captors subjected all the men to torture, to try to extract information of use to the Japanese intelligence service. Clearly even at this late stage of the war the enemy entertained no thoughts of eventual defeat. The four non-commissioned officers including Flight Sergeant Woodbridge, were separated and taken by motor transport to a forest, where they were beheaded.

The story of this atrocity only came to light later, in a war crimes trial. Three officers and three non-commissioned officers of the Japanese army were brought to trial by a military court, charged with the torture and murder of the four aircrew. All these Japanese were found guilty. Three were hanged and three sentenced to terms of imprisonment.

The trial revealed the details of the last days of the airmen. The Japanese concentrated their efforts on Woodbridge, in an endeavour to get technical information about wireless equipment, secret codes, wavelengths and any other useful facts which might have been known to a wireless operator.

A Japanese officer, with a technical background, had the job of interrogating Woodbridge. The services of two interpreters were also utilized. But in spite of repeated kicking, beating with belts, and beating with a sword, Woodbridge gave nothing away to the interrogator.

The final interrogation took place at the site of execution, when it was clear to the prisoner that he was to be put to death. Even so, he maintained his courageous attitude, only remarking that if the Japanese were going to kill him, they should do it quickly. Flight Sergeant Woodbridge was beheaded on 7 February 1945, one week after the Liberator crashed.

Havildar Abdul Rahman,
INDIAN ARMY

Java, 22 February 1945: an Indian Army jeep was on the move at Kletek carrying six soldiers of the 3rd Battalion, 9th Jat Regiment. The vehicle suddenly struck a mine on the road, careered off the track, and caught fire. The jeep somersaulted into the ditch running beside the road, trapping three of the six troops beneath it.

Havildar Rahman at once attempted to free them, but ammunition still aboard the jeep started to go off. Despite the deadly risk, Hahman dragged two of the trio clear. As he was in the act of rescuing the remaining man, the Javanese air was rent by the sound and sight of the jeep's fuel tanks exploding. Their blast caught Rahman, but he somehow shouted to the occupants of an ambulance to carry on with the rescue.

A moment or two later, Rahman died.

Lance Corporal David Russell,
22ND BATTALION, 2ND NEW ZEALAND EXPEDITIONARY FORCE

Scots-born New Zealander Lance Corporal Russell was taken a prisoner of war in Italy, but during 1943 he managed to get away from the camp, acquire non-incriminating clothes and merge into the local Italian community nearby. Under the watchful eye of a friendly peasant, Russell kept in touch with other prisoners who had also got away from the camp. This went on for two entire years, until the early days of 1945. Russell actually lived in the same house as the Italian peasant and it seemed as if he would be fortunate enough to evade attention and re-capture.

But in February 1945, a combined patrol of Germans and Italians arrested both men; Russell for being a prisoner of war and the peasant for sheltering him. They beat Russell to try to force him to admit knowing the peasant, but he managed to convince them that he did not. Perhaps surprisingly, they let the peasant go free.

However, the Germans felt sure that Russell knew of other escaped prisoners, as well as Italian partisans. In an effort to elicit names and locations, they chained Russell to a wall, beat him repeatedly and gave him just three days to disclose what they wanted to know. They made it clear to him that the alternative would be death. Russell refused to comply and was shot on 28 February 1945.

Albert Edward Heming,
CIVIL DEFENCE RESERVE SERVICE, BERMONDSEY

London was still suffering from the air only two months before the end of the war in Europe. On 2 March 1945, a Roman Catholic church and some houses were wrecked in Bermondsey. The resulting mêlée of bricks, stonework and an assortment of other materials trapped several people under its weight. In this particular house, four walls pancaked with the contents of the rooms sandwiched between them.

When Albert Heming and his section of the local Civil Defence

Rescue Service reached the scene, someone told them that two women and several priests could be among the pile of ruins. The likelihood of anyone still surviving seemed remote, but then a man's voice came from the crypt. Heming and his helpers burrowed towards the voice, eventually tracing the owner of the voice.

Debris and furniture completely encased the man, some of it supporting the floor above. By slow and patient work, Heming chiselled his way down through the mass of beams, masonry and plaster. Working head downwards, he removed the debris and furniture around the victim. Finally he found the man pinned down by a main timber which was fixed to a floor. Any movement of this beam would have precipitated a complete collapse of the structure surrounding the man and Heming, with fatal results to them both.

Despite the apparent hopelessness of the whole predicament, coupled with the added danger from coal gas escaping from a damaged pipe, Heming plodded on. Still upside down, he painstakingly picked off the matter covering the man until, after three hours, he managed to release him.

From the outset, it had appeared impossible to rescue this man, a Roman Catholic priest, but Heming refused to recognize this or abandon him. As in so many such rescues, it had seemed beyond human strength, but although the victim was badly hurt, he survived, entirely due to Albert Heming. The fact that the man was a priest could be considered as deeply symbolic of some forces beyond earthly understanding.

Lance Naik Islam-ud-Din,
INDIAN ARMY

This hero belonged to the 6/9th Jat Regiment of the Indian Army, serving in the Central Burma front of the Far East war. His typical Indian courage had already been noticed when he was in action against the Japanese on 24 March. 1945. The location of this encounter was Khanda, north of Meiktila. Less than three weeks later, he and his regimental comrades were at Pyawbwe. The

111

fateful date was 12 April, when a live grenade threatened to cause many casualties among the Indian troops. Rather than risk this, Islam-ud-Din cloaked it with his whole body, so that when it went off seconds later, it killed him but none of the others.

Lieutenant George Gosse,
ROYAL AUSTRALIAN NAVAL VOLUNTEER RESERVE

Will-o'-the-wisp George Gosse was awarded his George Cross for an exploit on, of all dates in history, 8 May 1945 – VE-Day! He had already risked his life many times before that while tackling enemy mines.

While clearing the docks and waterways at Bremen on VE-Day, Gosse was destined to tackle an 'unsweepable oyster' mine. Other divers had located the position of this mine, which they did not recognize as any known kind. Gosse went down and did recognize it as a famous, or infamous, 'oyster' pressure mine. The war in Europe might just be over, but it was still important to get hold of this mine and also to clear the Bremen waterways for future Allied naval movements.

Gosse decided that his initial effort at recovery and making safe should be where the mine lay – under water. He went down next morning and withdrew the primer. Remember, the slightest change in water pressure around the mine was the trigger for it to explode. It did not go off, but there was a distinct detonation-like sound. The conclusion was that if Gosse had tried to go through the conventional routine and tackled the fuse first, it would have erupted.

When a mine was being dealt with under water, the diver was obviously in a doubly dangerous situation. Any mishap at once became lethal. The diver could be killed by explosive or drowned as a result of its effects. Gosse and his support team later organized lifting the 'oyster' from the depths of Bremen harbour to a quay. Here he was able to investigate the circuitry at his comparative ease, although ease was a relative terms when applied to rendering safe any mine.

Two other 'oyster' mines were then discovered lying near the main channels to and from Bremen. George Gosse spent a proportion of the following ten days tackling these mines. The experience he gained from the original one helped him make them both harmless. As soon as the primer had been extracted, the detonator went off, too, before either mine had been brought clear of the water. His citation referred to Gosse's courage and skill. Good fortune might well have been added to those attributions.

Wing Commander Forest Frederick Edward Yeo-Thomas,
ROYAL AIR FORCE VOLUNTEER RESERVE

Sometimes the unadorned facts can convey experiences more convincingly than any attempt to embroider them. This is very true in the case of 'The White Rabbit'. Wing Commander Yeo-Thomas had this code-name when he was parachuted into France in February 1943. This was, in fact, only his first mission, but one in which he immediately showed courage and initiative.

A French officer was being followed by a Gestapo agent in Paris. Yeo-Thomas helped him to evade the German, reach safety and resume clandestine work in another area, where the man was not suspected. Yeo-Thomas next took charge of the plight of a US Army Air Corps officer who had been shot down and spoke no French, so was in imminent danger of being discovered. The American officer returned to England on 15 April 1943, actually in the same aircraft that picked up Yeo-Thomas on completion of his first mission. For many men, this would have been enough.

Yeo-Thomas volunteered for his second mission on 17 September of the same year. Soon after he arrived in France, many patriots were arrested. Undeterred, Yeo-Thomas got the information he needed to remedy the desperate situation. Six times during this second mission he barely escaped arrest by the Gestapo. They were also watching a house containing crucial British intelligence archives. Unperturbed by this, the White Rabbit managed to get these archives away from the vulnerable house and bring them back to England on 15 November 1943.

In February 1944, Yeo-Thomas was parachuted into France for the third time. Security precautions had been improved since his

113

earlier sorties, but on 21 March 1944 he was betrayed to the Gestapo by someone either in, or connected to, the French Resistance. While being taken by car to Gestapo headquarters, Yeo-Thomas was badly beaten up. Worse followed. He sustained four days of continuous interrogation, interspersed with beatings and torture. The latter included immersion, head downwards, in ice-cold water with his legs and arms chained

Interrogations later continued for two months and Yeo-Thomas was offered his freedom in return for information concerning the head of a Resistance secretariat. He remained silent. Owing to his wrist being cut by chains, Yeo-Thomas contracted blood poisoning and nearly lost his left arm. At this time, too, he made two daring, but unsuccessful, attempts to escape. After these, his captors confined him in solitude at Fresnes prison for four months, including three weeks in a darkened cell with hardly any food. Throughout these months of regular torture, Yeo-Thomas still refused to disclose any information.

On 11 July 1944, Wing Commander Yeo-Thomas was sent with a party to Compiegne prison. Twice more he tried to escape. He and thirty-six other prisoners were then transferred to Buchenwald. En route, they stopped for three days at Saarbrücken, where the Germans beat them and kept them in a tiny hut. They arrived at Buchenwald on 16 August, where sixteen of them were executed and cremated on 10 September.

Yeo-Thomas had already started to organize resistance within the camp, although conscious all the time that a similar fate could befall him. He took an opportunity of changing his identity with that of a dead French prisoner, on condition that other officers could also do so. In this way he was directly instrumental in saving the lives of two officers.

Later on, the Germans transferred him to a work commando for Jews. Here again he tried to escape, but was picked up by a German patrol. Claiming French nationality, he was transferred to a camp near Marienburg for French prisoners of war.

The war in Europe was nearing its finale. On 16 April 1945, Yeo-Thomas led a group of twenty in a broad-daylight attempt at escape. Half were killed by fire from the guards. Those who reached cover split up into small groups. The Wing Commander became separated from his companions after three days without food. He continued alone for a week, only to be retaken when a mere 800 yards from the American Army lines. The sands of time were down to the dregs for the Germans.

A few days later, Yeo-Thomas escaped with a party of ten French prisoners of war, and led them through enemy patrols to the American lines. Contrary to all odds, Wing Commander Yeo-Thomas survived to savour victory. To the George Cross, France added the Légion d'Honneur and Croix de Guerre. The White Rabbit also received the Cross of Merit from Poland.

Mrs Sansom: Odette Marie Celine,
WOMEN'S TRANSPORT SERVICE (FANY)

Odette – another legendary name in the SOE. She was infiltrated into enemy-occupied France in October 1942 and worked with great courage and distinction until the following April, when she was arrested with her commanding officer, Peter Churchill. Between Marseilles and Paris on their way to prison at Fresnes, she succeeded in speaking to Churchill. For mutual protection, they agreed to maintain that they were married. She adhered to this fiction and even succeeded in convincing her captors, despite considerable evidence to the contrary. This was sustained through at least fourteen interrogations.

She also drew Gestapo attention on to herself, saying that her 'husband' had only come to France on her insistence. She took full responsibility and agreed that it should be herself and not Churchill who should be shot. By this ploy, she caused the Gestapo to cease paying attention to him after only two of their interrogations.

In addition, the Gestapo were most determined to discover the whereabouts of a wireless operator and of another British officer, whose lives were of the greatest value to the Resistance organization. Mrs Sansom was the only person who knew of their location.

The Gestapo tortured her brutally. They seared her back with a red hot iron and, when that failed, they pulled out all her toenails.

115

Odette continually refused to speak. By her unbelievable stoicism in the face of such barbarism, she not only saved the lives of the two officers but also enabled them to carry on their vital work.

Odette was kept in solitary confinement for two years, showing continued courage. They moved her to Ravensbrück concentration camp and while there she was imprisoned in total darkness for three months and eleven days. The pretext for this punishment was in retaliation for the Allied invasion of southern France in August 1944. In the end, Odette was taken by the German camp Commandant to the advancing American Army in May 1945, when it had become clear that the war in Europe was at an end. As well as the George Cross, Odette later received the Légion d'Honneur in recognition of her service for France.

Lieutenant Commander Patrick Albert O'Leary,
ROYAL NAVY

Lieutenant Commander O'Leary was actually an assumed name. When war broke out in 1939, he was really Albert Marie Edmond Guerisse, a Belgian Army doctor. On the fall of his country in 1940, he got away to England and became an officer in the Royal Navy. He was given the name of O'Leary for his role of infiltrating Allied agents into France.

However in 1941 Vichy French police caught him while he was engaged on a landing operation near the coast of France. While being taken to a French prison for interrogation, O'Leary escaped. Somehow he established an organization to try to aid the rescue of prisoners of war and others. Under his leadership, the group grew to cope with the success of the network. O'Leary made a number of journeys from the borders of occupied Holland to the south of France, serving as the escort for various escaping prisoners.

This rescue work continued until March 1943. Then, an ever present risk became a reality when one of his own group gave him away to the Gestapo. They tortured him over a long period to try to extract names of his accomplices, their locations, their activities, and any facts. O'Leary did not reveal anything. Following this, they wrought what has been referred to as 'ferocious experiments' on him with the same refusal to talk.

Subsequently, O'Leary was subjected to yet further torture in concentration camps. His list of camps were Mauthausen, Natzweiler, Neubremm and Dachau. Miraculously, he survived all this, to be freed from the infamous Dachau along with other inmates.

From start to finish, the group formed by O'Leary was credited with the direct rescue of more than 600 Allied officers and men, over 250 of whom were saved personally by O'Leary. Among his many decorations, O'Leary was honoured by Belgium, France, Poland, the United States, and of course by Britain with the George Cross, and the Distinguished Service Order. Continuing his career, he served in Korea and was eventually Director General of the Medical Service, Belgian Forces.

Frederick Davies,
FIREMAN, NATIONAL FIRE SERVICE

Sometimes there is a tragic irony in real life that surpasses any fiction. Men of No. 34 (London) Area, National Fire Service, celebrated VJ-Day, along with the rest of the Allies. Then exactly one week later, on 22 August 1945, a shop and five-room house in Harlesden, London, caught fire.

Frederick Davies was one of the firemen called to the premises, then fiercely alight. The NFS were told: 'There are two children in the front room on the second floor.'

The severity of the flames precluded the possibility of any rescue via the ground floor. So the escape ladder was immediately pitched to the middle window of the second storey. Even before his colleagues could put it in final position, Davies ran up its lower rungs.

At this stage, flames were spurting from the upper floor and also licking up the front of the building. Reaching the window, Davies tried to force his way inside, but a burst of flame halted him. Undaunted, he clambered through the window with his back to the blaze. The men below watched while he tried to remove his

117

tunic, presumably to wrap around the children. But his hands were already too badly burned for him to do so.

During this time, Davies was moving around the internal inferno to locate the two children. In a few minutes, he returned with one child in his arms. He handed this youngster out of the window to a waiting fireman. His officer ordered him to descend the ladder, but Davies ignored this and turned back into the room to find the second child.

The next sight of him from below came when he flung himself from the window-ledge on to the ladder, with the whole of his clothing alight. The other child was probably already dead when he bore her down the escape ladder. He was helped to the ground, his scorching attire was extinguished and they rushed him to hospital suffering from severe burns. When he had reached the ground, someone said he was 'a human torch'. Not surprisingly, Davies died from his injuries – a peacetime casualty.

Captain Mahmood Khan Durrani,
INDIAN STATE FORCES

When Malaya was being overrun by the Japanese in 1942, Captain Durrani was cut off with a group of his 1st Bahawalpur Infantry. They managed to evade discovery for some three months and were only caught as a result of betrayal to the enemy-sponsored Indian Nationalist Army. After being dispatched to a prisoner of war camp, Durrano withstood attempts to make him join this Nationalist force. More than that, he did all he could to intercept enemy plans to infiltrate Nationalists into India itself.

Durrano achieved his objective for a while, but later in the war – just before D-Day – the enemy started to inflict terrible torture on him to try to force him to reveal the names of his helpers in his activities, preventing the subversion of Indian prisoners. As the Japanese could not get Durrani to talk, they transferred him to the charge of the Nationalist forces. Imprisoned by his own countrymen, he suffered further torture before they condemned him to death. However, with Durrani continuing to resist and with the war ending, the liberation of all prisoners brought about the miracle of release from suffering. Despite his ordeal, Durrani had somehow survived.

Naik Kirpa Ram,
INDIAN ARMY

This was yet another incident involving grenades. Naik Ram belonged to the 8th Battalion 13th Frontier Force Rifles, of the Indian Army. On 12 September 1945, the war had already been won. That was the supreme irony of this accident.

Kirpa Ham was in charge of a field exercise of firing grenades from a discharger. He had his men close to him when a sepoy started to fire. One of the grenades fell a few yards from the other men in Kirpa Ram's section. An imminent explosion would be bound to cause casualties. Kirpa Ram ran towards the grenade, as he warned the men to take cover. He got hold of it, hoping to hurl it to a safe spot. But before he could do so, the grenade blasted off. The result of the accident was the death of Naik Kirpa Ram. The only other casualties caused were to two men who suffered slight wounds. He had saved lives while losing his own. This was the epitaph of too many men who sacrificed themselves in similar circumstances.

Chapter Seven

1946

Major Kenneth Alfred Biggs,
ROYAL ARMY ORDNANCE CORPS
Staff Sergeant Sidney George Rogerson,
ROYAL ARMY ORDNANCE CORPS

Members of the Royal Army Ordnance Corps are always aware of the chance of an accident when they are near explosive materials.

The first year of peace opened quietly in Wiltshire. Then on 2 January 1946, Major Biggs and Staff Sergeant Rogerson were among the officers and men of the RAOC, Pioneer Corps, and Royal Army Service Corps loading a train with both American and German ammunition in Savernake Forest, Wiltshire. Alongside this train in the siding stood a second one filled with British ammunition. The total number of trucks numbered ninety-six. Something caused a flash, followed by an immediate outburst – like lightning before thunder. Two of the wagons and a large lorry vanished; fire tore through the goods yard and the number of trucks afire multiplied. A succession of explosions disposed of twenty-seven rail wagons and two lorries, with the distinct risk that the whole yard would be destroyed, with consequent havoc and loss of life. The original explosion had already claimed the lives of eight soldiers, while a further six lay hurt.

At this critical stage, Major Biggs and Staff Sergeant Rogerson jointly uncoupled one wagon and put out the fire threatening its lethal load. The explosions went on regularly, and the powerful

120

blast from one of these battered Biggs to the ground. Still shaken, he got up and went on directing his soldiers in the urgent need to try to stop the spread of fire. By going on nonstop throughout the night, they averted what seemed almost inevitable. No further ammunition wagons became alight or exploded.

Dawn on 3 January revealed the remains of rail wagons, Army vehicles, mines and shells, not to mention a mélange of detonators, packages and even felled telegraph poles. The Wiltshire landscape was littered with matter from the accident, and further pitted by two colossal craters. However, the heroic achievement of Major Biggs and Staff Sergeant Rogerson, plus all the other rescuers, was that out of those original ninety-six wagons, they had saved sixty-nine.

Driver Joseph Hughes,
ROYAL ARMY SERVICE CORPS

Self-sacrifice in Hong Kong. This sums up the life and death of Driver Hughes. The date was 21 March 1946 and the Colony of Hong Kong had more or less returned to a peacetime routine. Hughes was at the wheel of his lorry heading into Lyemum barracks. The three-tonner was transporting a load of explosives to the magazine store at the barracks. All had the appearance of a normal day.

Suddenly, a smouldering somewhere on the lorry turned to fire. Hughes had two choices; he could either hurry a safe distance from an impending explosion, or try to avert it. He chose the latter. He grabbed the fire extinguisher and started to spray the fire. Next, he pulled burning netting away from the vehicle, while calling to all within range of danger to get as far as possible from the fire. His double action of combating the blaze and ensuring that other people were safe certainly avoided casualties amomg them. Then all the ammunition aboard the lorry erupted into a shattering sequence of sound and fury.

Driver Hughes died on the spot.

Squadron Leader Hubert Dinwoodie,
ROYAL AIR FORCE VOLUNTEER RESERVE

Bombs did not distinguish between war and peace; nor between Britain and Germany. The next location for bomb disposal was at the port of Lübeck in Germany on 20 August 1946. German high explosive bombs were being loaded into vessels at Lübeck for safe disposal at sea. Two trainloads of bombs, weighing over 1,000 tons altogether, were drawn into the quayside.

As usual, care was being taken during the process of loading into the waiting barges. This progressed normally until the German loading party accidentally dropped a 50-kilogram bomb a distance of about four feet. The bomb was fitted with a 'tel' fuse, and was one of a batch of twelve being handled at the same time.

The bomb hit the quay and went off, killing outright six persons and injuring twelve. Worse than this, the immediate danger was that one or more of the eleven remaining bombs would also detonate; possibly the whole trainload would go up. The decision had to be taken to summon a bomb disposal party to deal with the situation. Squadron Leader Dinwoodie was a member of an RAF Bomb Disposal Squadron stationed in Germany. He was sent urgently to Lübeck to report on the current situation and to clear the dangerous missiles.

Starting this hazardous job, Dinwoodie discovered that the remaining eleven bombs, similar to the dropped one, were an experimental type, fitted with a special shock-sensitive, electrically-operated fuse. Corporal Roland Garred had been detailed as an assistant to the Squadron Leader, and together they had the task of taking 'appropriate action' to safeguard the munitions train, not themselves.

Dinwoodie and Garred proceeded to tackle the first of the eleven bombs. The fuse had already been damaged in the original explosion. The two men worked in an atmosphere of extreme tension. They knew nothing about the cause of the explosion, nor whether their action of defusing the bomb would, itself, result in another detonation – and death.

Furthermore, in view of the length of time that these bombs had been in storage, the state of their main fillings was not above suspicion and sensitive exudation products might have formed around the main tube. If so, the moment they removed the tube could cause detonation.

With infinite care, Dinwoodie and Garred tackled bomb number one, which they managed to defuse. They found that the probable cause of the accident had been defective design or workmanship. Moving on to several other bombs of the eleven confirmed that the fusing device had already moved, rendering the bomb dangerous. All eleven bombs were made safe and from the information obtained it became possible to minimize the danger and clear the trains.

The docks at Lübeck were close to the historic town, so Dinwoodie and Garred avoided the devastation and casualties that would have been inevitable if the trains had exploded. An official called their action 'cold-blooded heroism'.

Throughout the long operation, Dinwoodie and Garred had the help of Leading Aircraftman John Hatton. He had been detailed to assist them as motor transport support when required. From the night of 20 August until they had cleared the bombs, Hatton did all that was asked of him, knowing he was working alongside loaded munitions trains and adjacent to eleven bombs which were all in a shock-sensitive state.

When it became vital to move a damaged rail wagon, still laden with the remainder of the bombs, Hatton towed it cautiously along the dockside until it had been manoeuvred into the desired position. During the whole hazardous time, Hatton was a member of the bomb disposal party, operating within the danger area. He was always at hand and eager to help when it was needed.

In the final phase of the operation, Hatton and Dinwoodie alone transported the eleven bombs to a demolition site, Hatton doing his share of the work involved in blowing them up. Four days were needed to complete the whole job. Hatton and his vehicle were ready all the time, loaded with the appropriate stores and in perfect condition.

Clearing these potentially lethal munitions depended on very exact movements and perfectly timed teamwork. Dinwoodie was the first to recognize the crucial contribution made by both Garred and Hatton. The respective awards made to the three men were: Squadron Leader Dinwoodie, George Cross; Corporal Garred, George Medal; Leading Aircraftman Hatton, British Empire Medal.

During the preceding year, from August 1945 to August 1946, Dinwoodie and Garred defused dangerous bombs in considerable quantities. Dinwoodie was responsible for the clearing and demolition of large dumps of German bombs, many of them in a highly unstable state.

Chapter Eight

1947

Able Seaman Thomas Raymond Kelly

The date: 18 March 1947. The place: the Bay of Biscay. This next epic episode is bound to be a story of the sea. While the SS *Famagusta* of London was on a voyage to Cyprus, she encountered severe weather in the bay. The spring wind whipped to gale force in squalls and the seas ran high and tumbling. Not surprisingly, the steamship started to list to port. As the weather worsened by the hour, her list increased and she began shipping water.

The situation appeared so serious to the captain of the *Famagusta* that an SOS went out across the radio waves. Fortunately the route was a regular one to the Mediterranean and the SS *Empire Plover* of London responded and stood by. The *Empire Plover* was a ship of the Ormos Shipping Company. Circumstances had clearly reached a May Day state, because the *Famagusta* launched a lifeboat which started to try to pull towards the *Empire Plover*. Amid the fury of the Bay of Biscay the lifeboat capsized and hurled its ten occupants into the sea.

Despite the waters seething all around the *Empire Plover*, the steamship quickly manoeuvred into position and lowered rescue ropes, ladders and scrambling nets. Three of her crew actually stripped and entered the water, two of them managing to remain at the nets and ladders, ready to help rescue survivors. The third of the trio, Able Seaman Thomas Kelly, from County Down, swam off with a line towards the crew of the lifeboat, who were by then battling in the raging sea.

First of all, Kelly brought a badly injured officer to safety. He then swam out again and returned with a second member of the *Famagusta*'s crew. After ensuring this man's survival and safety, he swam off a third time, on this occasion to the aid of a woman, seen to be struggling some fifty yards away. Kelly succeeded in reaching her, but both of them were at that moment struck by a sea still heavier than encountered so far. Kelly and the woman disappeared. Tragically, too, five others of the ten in the lifeboat were also drowned. But without question, Kelly had saved the lives of the officer and one other crew member.

Sergeant John Archibald Beckett,
ROYAL AIR FORCE

It should have been a routine refuelling operation. On the night of 28 March 1947, the Royal Air Force were replenishing a Lancaster aircraft of 38 Squadron at the RAF Station of Ein Shemer, Air Headquarters, Levant. For some unknown reason, violent fire broke out in the pumping compartment of the refuelling vehicle which was being driven by Sergeant John Beckett.

The flames enveloped Beckett and set alight the front of the fuselage of the Lancaster. Although another airman rapidly beat out the flames on Beckett, he had already sustained bad burns to his hands and face; the exposed areas of his body.

At this moment, the main tank of the vehicle could well have exploded, together with its contents of 2,000 gallons of fuel. Had this happened most, if not all, of the twenty surrounding aircraft would have been destroyed.

Beckett had serious and painful injuries, but instantly got into the driver's seat of the blazing vehicle and drove it some 400 yards to a point beyond the aircraft park, where it could do no further damage. As in other comparable actions, having achieved what he had set out to do, Becket collapsed quickly. An ambulance rushed in the wake of his refuelling vehicle and took him to the station sick quarters, dangerously ill.

The fires in the Lancaster and the vehicle were eventually brought under control and extinguished, without further damage to persons or property. So Beckett saved not only his comrades from the risk of injury, but many aircraft from damage or destruction. The price exacted for this proved too high. Sergeant Beckett died of his injuries a fortnight after the accident.

Chapter Nine

1950s

Robert George Taylor,
NEWSPAPER ADVERTISING REPRESENTATIVE

No one knows how long, or short, a time they will live. On 13 March 1950, Robert Taylor was in his thirtieth year, so would be expecting to live for a long while.

Two armed men entered a sub-branch of Lloyds Bank in Bristol. They threatened the cashier and bank guard with a revolver, stole a large wad of money and escaped. The alarm was raised and the two men ran off at some speed over open land.

Robert Taylor, a newspaper advertising representative, decided on impulse to take up the chase. He caught up with the man who was carrying the gun and tried to grapple with him. But the bank robber, alarmed, turned and fired point-blank into Taylor's face. The injuries inflicted proved fatal. Taylor had acted out of an urge and desire to help preserve law and order. He did not pause to consider any possible cost. So 13 March 1950 proved to be the last day of his short life.

Aircraftman 1st Class Ivor John Gillett,
ROYAL AIR FORCE, FAR EAST FLYING BOAT WING, SELETAR

A Sunderland flying boat blew up at its moorings on the Royal Air Force Flying Boat Base, Seletar, on 26 March 1950. Seletar was one of the three RAF bases on Singapore, the other two being Changi and Tengah. As a fitter armourer, Aircraftman 1st Class Ivor Gillett was a member of the ground crew on board the Sunderland at the time.

Rescue surface craft reached the scene quickly, but the flying boat and a bomb scow alongside both sank rapidly. Survivors from the explosion were tipped into the warm water lapping Singapore. A crew member of a rescue launch tossed a lifebelt to Gillett, but he was seen to throw this to a seriously injured corporal. This non-commissioned officer was near to Gillett and in imminent danger of drowning. In the confusion, the rescuers were unable to reach this man. Gillett was a great friend of the corporal and knew he was not a strong swimmer. Injured, he would have not survived. In the event, the lifebelt kept the corporal afloat until he was rescued, unconscious, from the water some minutes later.

In the vital interim time, Gillett disappeared. Two days elapsed before his body was washed ashore on Singapore. Then they discovered that he, too, had suffered injuries and that his death had been due to the combined effects of the original shock from the blast and ultimately of drowning. As a personal footnote, I remembered Ivor Gillett while on duty at nearby RAF Changi a decade later . . .

George Anthony Taylor,
VULCANOLOGIST

Mount Lamington in Papua began to rumble into volcanic life on the night of 18 January 1951. Three days later, on Sunday 21 January, the Volcano erupted with violence, blowing away a large part of the northern side of the mountain. Steam hissed and smoke puffed from the gap for a long time afterwards.

The area of maximum devastation extended over a radius of about eight miles from the volcano, while people near Higaturu, nine miles away, were killed by the blast or burned to death. Before this and subsequent eruptions subsided, some 4,000 people had died and much havoc ensued.

129

George Taylor was a vulcanologist with the Commonwealth Bureau of Mineral Resources, Territory of Papua and New Guinea. He arrived at Mount Lamington on the Monday after the initial eruption. From that day onwards for several months, Taylor displayed courage in the close proximity of the violent volcano. He visited the crater almost daily, either by aircraft or on foot.

This was the scene that confronted Taylor from the very first. Dust and ash filled every stream and tank for miles around. There was the familiar urgent call for food, water and medical supplies. Rescue parties were hampered by the suffocating pumice and sulphurous fumes, as well as the hot ashes actually covering much of the ground.

Sometimes Taylor stayed at the foot of the volcano throughout the night. During the whole of this protracted period, the volcano was never entirely quiescent. Several times the earth erupted without any warning whatsoever, or any prior indication from the seismological data which Taylor had collected, when not otherwise engaged in emergency rescue work.

The advance post of relief workers at Popondetta was threatened with destruction by the subsequent eruptions over the days following 21 January. Further tremors and explosions rumbled and roared on into February and throughout that month. And as late as 5 March, six weeks and more after 21 January, another major upthrust threw chunks of volcanic substance as far as two miles from the epicentre. These vast volcanic pieces measured 15 feet by 12 feet by 10 feet. They caused a flow of lava and rocks for a distance of nine miles, while the whole moving mass was so hot that it set fire to every tree unlucky enough to happen to be standing in its inexorable path.

It is impossible to cover all that George Taylor achieved, both in his professional and personal capacity. Without worrying about his own skin at any time, he went into the most dangerous area of the eruptions again and again. On each occasion, he had his twin role of ensuring the safety of the rescue and working parties, and also of gathering urgent scientific information about this type of volcano. Little was known hitherto of its possible behaviour pattern.

In retrospect it was established that Taylor saved many lives. And as a result of his work in the maximum danger zone, he was able to warn rehabilitation parties to avoid hazardous areas, where he had fearlessly gone himself.

Lieutenant Terence Edward Waters

The Korean War. At the battle of the Imjin River, Lieutenant Terence Waters was an officer in the West Yorkshire Regiment (The Prince of Wales's Own), attached to the Gloucestershire Regiment. During the early stages of this battle, Waters sustained an injury in the top of his head and another painful wound to an arm. He was subsequently captured by the Chinese communists.

Forced to march to Pyungyang with other prisoners of war, Waters set a wonderful example by staying with wounded of other ranks of soldiers, whom he did his best to care for and comfort. This was in spite of his own serious wounds.

After an infamous march of immense hardship and privation, the prisoner of war party arrived at an area west of Pyungyang, adjacent to prison camp 12. The area was known generally as The Caves and this turned out to be where they would be held captive. They found themselves imprisoned in a tunnel driven into a hillside, through which a stream of water flowed continuously. This flooded a great deal of the floor where many South Korean and European prisoners were kept. They were already in rags, filthy, and crawling with lice.

In this cavernous hell, a number of prisoners died daily from wounds, sickness, or merely malnutrition. They were fed two small meals of boiled maize daily, and received no medical attention. Lieutenant Waters realized that few, if any, of them would survive such conditions for long.

A North Korean political officer visited and tried to persuade them to volunteer to join a prisoner of war group known as Peace Fighters – that is, active participants in the propaganda movement against their own side. If they were to do this, they were promised better food, medical care and other amenities as a reward. The prisoners refused the offer unanimously.

131

However, Lieutenant Waters could see that they would not live long unless something were done to help them. Accordingly, he decided to order his men to pretend to accept this offer. He issued the necessary instructions to the senior non-commissioned officer with the British party, Sergeant Hoper.

Waters realized that this act would save many lives in his party, but he refused to go himself, knowing that maintaining British prestige was vested in him. The North Koreans then made a series of concerted efforts to persuade Waters to save himself by joining the Peace Fighters. But they could not subvert him and he refused to give way. He was a young, inexperienced officer, who had been comparatively recently commissioned from the Royal Military Academy at Sandhurst. Nevertheless, he set an example of mature gallantry. He died shortly afterwards.

George Campbell Henderson,
SUB OFFICER, GIBRALTAR DOCKYARD FIRE SERVICE

Under the shadow of the Rock of Gibraltar, a lighter caught fire in the famous harbour. The date was 27 April 1951, just before the opening of the Festival of Britain. The lighter was laden with explosives and ammunition, and lay alongside the naval armament vessel *Bedenham*. Sub Officer Henderson was in charge of the first fire appliance sent to fight the conflagration – already virtually out of control.

The blistering heat and intensity of flames were bound to cause some sort of violent explosion of ammunition at any moment. Nevertheless, Henderson clambered aboard the *Bedenham* and managed to direct a jet of water into the lighter. He stood immediately alongside and above the blazing vessel. By then the order had been received to abandon the *Bedenham*, but Henderson stood securely at his chosen vantage point, together with his fire hose.

He continued doing what he could to prevent an explosion, knowing that this must come and that when it did, his chance of survival would be slight. The inevitable did happen a short while later. The whole ammunition aboard the lighter blew up in a

shattering sequence of sound. Henderson was killed at once. He
had shown that high degree of courage associated with a fire
officer's job.

Awang anak Rawang,
IBAN TRACKER, JOHORE, FEDERATION OF MALAYA

Malaya, May 1951. During operations against bandits in Malaya,
a section of a platoon of the Worcestershire Regiment was
ambushed by about fifty of the enemy. The bandits killed the
leading scout instantly, while the section commander was fatally
wounded. Awang anak Rawang was hit through the thigh bone.
At the same time, a soldier moving behind him was hit below the
knee; the bullet shattering the bone.

Although wounded and lying exposed under heavy rifle and
automatic fire, Awang anak Rawang collected his own weapons
and that of the soldier and dragged him into the cover of the
jungle. Anticipating an impending attack, Awang anak Rawang
took up a position to defend his injured comrade, disregarding his
own wound.

There he remained, firing on every attempt by the bandits to
approach them. He successfully repulsed several such attacks, but
ultimately and inevitably he was wounded once more. The bullet
that struck him shattered his right arm and rendered impossible
any further use of his rifle or parang.

He was still losing a lot of blood from his undressed wounds,
yet he dragged himself over to the wounded British soldier and
snatched a grenade from the man's pouch. He resumed his self-
appointed position on guard, pulled out the pin of the grenade
with, his teeth and, with the missile poised in his left hand, defied
the bandits to approach.

The enemy had been keeping up their attacks on the two men
for some forty minutes by this time, but Awang anak Rawang had
been equally resolute and determined for just as long. Then other
British sections of the Worcestershires began to threaten the
bandits so they withdrew. So Awang anak Rawang assuredly
saved the soldier's life, though being wounded severely twice and

losing blood continuously throughout the action. His citation spoke of his 'utmost courage'.

Flight Lieutenant John Alan Quinton, DFC,
RAF, 228 OPERATIONAL CONVERSION UNIT

On 13 August 1951, Flight Lieutenant Quinton was flying as a navigator under instruction in a Wellington aircraft. A sudden mid-air collision caused the Wellington to break up. Quinton and an Air Training Corps cadet passenger were in the rear compartment of the aircraft when the shock of the collision occurred. As the Wellington began plunging towards the ground out of control, Quinton snatched up the only parachute within his immediate reach and clipped it on to the cadet's harness.

He pointed to the ripcord of the parachute and also at a gaping hole in the aircraft fuselage – thereby indicating to the cadet that he should jump. At that second, a further portion of the Wellington was torn away and the cadet was literally flung through the side of the plane. Without time to decide whether or not to jump, he found himself clutching the ripcord; pulling it, and landing safely.

Quinton had acted with 'superhuman' speed and he knew that in giving up the only available parachute, he was forfeiting any chance of saving his own life. The Air Training Corps cadet was, in fact, the sole survivor of the tragic collision. Yet it was due entirely to Quinton's sacrifice that anyone at all was saved from the disaster.

Private Horace William Madden,
3RD BATTALION, ROYAL AUSTRALIAN REGIMENT

During the Korean War, the Chinese communists were just as brutal and barbarous as the Japanese in the Second World War. The Chinese took Private Madden prisoner on 24 April 1951 near Kapyong. They made frequent attempts to force him to collaborate, beating him regularly and subjecting him to further forms of savagery. He refused to change his attitude and did his best to keep a sense of cheerfulness – unbelievable as that might seem. The reputation of his heroic stance spread to all the other prisoners of war, inspiring them to withstand their incarceration at the hands of the communists. Gradually it became a battle of wills between Madden and his captors. Although he never wavered in his refusal to collaborate with them, the vile treatment inflicted on him made him progressively weaker over the ensuing months. The death of Private Madden on 6 November 1951 was finally attributed to lack of food allied to prolonged torture. No one can forgive this terrible treatment.

John Bamford,
COLLIERY WORKER

John Bamford was a fifteen-year-old colliery worker in 1952. On 19 Octotoer a fire broke out at his home in Nottinghamshire. The family consisted of his father, mother and six children including himself. Within minutes, in the early hours of that morning, the house began to burn strongly.

John went downstairs with his father, but when they opened the living room door, flames spurted and sprang from inside. The heat had by then cut them off from returning upstairs. The rest of the family were still all up there in jeopardy. John and Mr Bamford ran out through the front door, climbed on to the top of a downstairs bay window, and reached a bedroom window. They forced it open and helped three of the children and Mrs Bamford on to the roofing.

John and his father clambered almost headfirst through the bedroom window, where they could hear the two remaining children, aged four and six, shouting from the back bedroom. This room was situated right above the seat of the fire. The bedroom door at the head of the stair was alight. John's father draped a blanket around himself, but it caught fire and he was driven back by the heat.

John Bamford then told his father to go to the back of the house, while he got down on his hands and knees and started to

135

crawl through the flames into the children's bedroom. His shirt was completely burned on him, but he snatched his two young brothers from the bed and managed to get them across to the bedroom window. John dropped the four-year-old from the window actually into his father's arms below, but the elder boy struggled from John's grasp. The boy screamed as he ran through the fire across the room. John left the window and chased the lad, caught him, and literally threw him from the bedroom window.

By then, John Bamford was losing consciousness. He had terrible burns across the face, neck, chest, back, arms and hands. But somehow he managed to force one of his legs over the window-sill and then he fell to the ground, unconscious. His two brothers soon recovered, but John needed four months of skin grafts before he was well enough to rejoin his family. At the time of writing (in 2005) he is still the youngest person ever to be directly awarded the George Cross.

Detective Constable Frederick William Fairfax,
METROPOLITAN POLICE FORCE

Shortly after nine o'clock on the night of 24 November 1952, two youths were spotted climbing over the side gate of a warehouse at Croydon and reaching the flat roof of the building about twenty-two feet above.

The alarm reached the local police station and Detective Constable Fairfax, Police Constable Norman Harrison and other officers hurried to the premises in a van. At about the same time, Police Constable James McDonald and another officer arrived in a wireless car. Still other officers took up various strategic positions around the building.

When he heard that the suspects had climbed up a drainpipe to reach the roof, Fairfax immediately scaled the same pipe. McDonald followed him, but could not negotiate the final six feet to the top and had to return to the ground.

Fairfax reached the top alone and hauled himself on to the roof. In the moonlight, he saw the two youths outlined behind a brick chimney-stack. They were about fifteen yards away from him. He walked towards them, challenged them, and then dashed behind the stack and grabbed one of them. Fairfax pulled him into the open area of the roof, but the youth broke clear. The second youth then produced a gun and fired at Fairfax, wounding him in the right shoulder.

Fairfax fell to the ground with the shot, but as the two criminals ran past him to try and escape, the constable staggered up and closed with one of the pair, knocking him down. A second shot was then fired at Fairfax, but he somehow kept his hold on the youth, dragged him behind a skylight, and searched him. The policeman found a knuckleduster and a dagger, which he removed.

Meanwhile, McDonald had made another effort to climb the drainpipe and almost reached the top. Despite his wounds, Fairfax helped him on to the roof and called to the gunman to drop his weapon. The youth refused and made further threats.

During this time, Police Constable Harrison had climbed on to a sloping roof nearby and was edging his way along towards the gunman. He managed this by lying back on the roof with his heels in the guttering. But he was spotted and a shot was fired at him, which struck the roof close to his head. He went on, however, as another shot rang out and fortunately missed him. Harrison then got behind the shelter of a chimney-stack and reached the ground. Here he joined other officers who entered the building, ran up to the fire escape exit door, and pushed it open.

Fairfax called out a warning to them that the gunman was nearby, but one constable, Sidney Miles, jumped from the doorway on to the roof. As he did so, the gunman fired at the constable, who fell to the ground dead, shot between the eyes.

Fairfax at once left his cover to bring in the casualty, and yet another shot was aimed at him. McDonald also came forward and the two officers dragged the body of the constable behind the fire escape exit.

Harrison then jumped out on to the roof and, standing in the doorway, threw his truncheon and other objects at the gunman, who again fired at him. Police Constable Jaggs reached the roof by way of the drainpipe and was also subjected to gunfire but he managed to join the other constables.

Fairfax, still injured, helped Harrison, then pushed his captive through the doorway and handed the youth over to the other officers. Fairfax was given a police pistol and he returned to the roof. He leapt through the doorway and again called on the gunman to drop the weapon. Yet a further shot was fired at him, but he advanced towards the gunman, firing his own pistol as he went. The youth then jumped over the side of the roof to the ground below, where he was arrested.

All the police officers acted in their highest traditions. Fairfax repeatedly risked death and, although wounded, he would not give up until the criminals were seen to be safely in the charge of the police. Frederick Fairfax was awarded the George Cross; Norman Harrison, the George Medal and James McDonald and Robert Jaggs, the British Empire Medal. Fairfax was later promoted to detective sergeant.

The two young offenders were Derek Bentley and Christopher Craig. They were both charged with the murder of Police Constable Miles although it was Craig who fired the shot that killed him. Tried at the Old Bailey in December 1952 before the Lord Chief Justice, Lord Goddard, they were both found guilty. Craig, who was only sixteen, was sentenced to be detained at Her Majesty's Pleasure and served ten years in prison. Bentley, aged nineteen, was sentenced to death and was hanged on 28 January 1953. The events caused a public outcry and the case was depicted in a 1991 film entitled *Let Him Have It*.

Radio Officer David Broadfoot,
MERCHANT NAVY

With wintry seas running off Scotland, the motor vessel *Princess Victoria* left Stranraer on the morning of 31 January 1953, carrying 127 passengers for Larne.

After the comparative safety of Loch Ryan, she ran into north-westerly gales and squalls of sleet and snow. A particularly heavy sea struck the ship and burst open her stern doors. The foaming seawater flooded the whole space on the car deck, causing a list to starboard that reached ten degrees. Amid the dangerous gale, crewmen tried to secure the stern doors, but could not do so.

The Master then tried to turn his ship back to Loch Ryan, but the overall conditions of wind and water made the manoeuvre impossible. Some of the ship's cargo then started to shift from port to starboard – always an alarming sign in circumstances like these. This increased the original list from the car deck, as the crippled vessel endeavoured to plough her way across the turbulence of the Irish Sea.

From the moment when the *Princess Victoria* first got into difficulties, fifty-three-year-old Radio Officer David Broadfoot started to send out wireless messages constantly, giving the ship's current position and asking for urgent help. The severe and increased list of the vessel made his job more difficult than normal. Despite the danger threatening the whole complement of passengers and crew, Broadfoot went on at his transmitting set, repeatedly emitting signals to the coast radio station. These enabled the recipients to ascertain the ship's exact position as she lurched on towards Ireland.

When the *Princess Victoria* eventually stopped within sight of the Irish coast, her list had increased to 45 degrees. The vessel was practically on her beam ends. The Master gave the order: 'Abandon ship.'

Thinking only of saving the lives of the large number of people aboard, Broadfoot stayed in his wireless telegraphy cabin, sending and receiving more messages.

Meanwhile, the coastal tanker *Pass of Drumochter* heard over her radio of the *Princess Victoria*'s plight. Her Captain, James Kelly, put to sea immediately. As he passed the *Lairdsmoor*, he blew blasts on his ship's whistle to attract the attention of the Master of that vessel. Radio messages were also picked up by the *Orchy*. The *Lairdsmoor* had 100 head of cattle on board, while *Orchy* was practically in ballast and so vulnerable to the anger of the elements. But the Captains of each vessel put out to sea at once. They were, respectively, James Alexander Bell and Hugh Angus Matheson.

After leaving the shelter of Belfast Lough, the vessels were almost overwhelmed by the same heavy seas that had hit the *Princess Victoria*. And the same snow and sleet squalls as earlier, cut their visibility at times to nil. In company with *Orchy* and *Lairdsmoor*, the *Pass of Drumochter* swept the area by the Copelands for traces of the distressed ship.

Unknown to them, the *Princess Victoria* finally foundered. Then at 2.45 p.m., *Orchy* ran into boats and wreckage from the *Princess Victoria* and at once called the other ships to the scene.

Another rescue craft entered the story at that late stage. The trawler *Eastcotes* was sheltering in Belfast Lough when she heard the distress calls from the *Princess Victoria*, and that the 'Abandon Ship' order was about to be given. Her skipper, David Brewster, decided to weigh anchor and sail at speed, if possible, for the transmitted position. *Eastcotes* arrived at the location between 3 p.m. and 3.30 p.m., having been guided by *Orchy*, when the wreckage was seen.

The crew of *Eastcotes* were stationed on the deck ready to assist any survivors from buoyant apparatus or wreckage. Skipper Brewster was on the bridge alone, handling the ship in the storm-swept conditions. They managed to pick up one survivor and six bodies. After a sustained search until 6 p.m. and darkness, *Eastcotes* returned to her anchorage.

The weather was so appalling that none of the other rescue vessels could launch boats. Despite this maritime nightmare, they all went on trying to get survivors aboard their vessels. Meanwhile, the Donaghadee lifeboat, under Coxswain Hugh Nelson, and the Portpatrick lifeboat, under Coxswain William McConnell, were actually launched in a gale of hurricane force and into rough seas. The lifeboats reached the scene at 3.15 p.m and rescued thirty-three people from the ship's lifeboats and rafts. They went on searching for further survivors and the Donaghadee boat put out again at night and again at 7 a.m. on 1 February, searching the whole seascape until nightfall.

Throughout the worsening emergency, and with his cabin tilting halfway to the horizontal, Radio Officer Broadfoot remained on the *Princess Victoria*, knowing he would have no chance of survival. In making this supreme sacrifice, he was directly responsible for the rescuers reaching the doomed motor vessel and for saving the lives of those who did not perish in this tragedy. Many men took part in the ultimate rescues, but Radio

Officer Broadfoot went down with his ship on a night of the worst weather in the twentieth century.

Fusilier Derek Godfrey Kinne

The Korean war once more. In August 1950, Fusilier Derek Kinne volunteered for service in Korea. He joined the 1st Battaliom, The Royal Northumberland Fusiliers, and fought in the famous Imjin River battle. Kinne was captured by Chinese communists on 25 April 1951, the very last day of the battle.

From then on, he had only two objects in mind: firstly, to escape, and secondly to raise the morale of his fellow prisoners. Kinne had complete contempt for his captors and their behaviour, especially the treatment meted out to him. This was what happened to him after his capture.

Kinne escaped for the first time within twenty-four hours of becoming a prisoner, but was retaken a few days later while trying to get through to the British lines. Eventually he rejoined a large group of prisoners being marched north to a camp. Despite the hardship of this month-long march, Kinne rapidly emerged as a man of leadership and high morale.

July 1952 now. Kinne was well known to his captors, who accused him of being non-cooperative. He was brutally interrogated for information on other uncooperative prisoners of war, but he refused to give anything away about them.

As a result of striking back at a Chinese officer who had assaulted him, Kinne was severely beaten twice. Then he was tied up for continuous periods of twelve and twenty-four hours. While in this state, he was forced to stand on tiptoe with a running noose around his neck, which would have throttled him if he had tried to relax in any way. Torture of an evil kind.

Kinne actually escaped on 27 July 1952, but was recaptured, this time within two days. The Chinese once more beat him up viciously. They then put him in handcuffs, frequently applying tightening pressure on his wrists to restrict circulation. Kinne was kept in handcuffs until 16 October 1952, a period of eighty-one days.

From August onwards, he was accused of having a hostile attititude towards the Chinese; sabotage of compulsory political study; escaping and of being a reactionary. From 15–20 August, the Chinese confined him in a very small box cell. Here he was made to sit to attention all day. Periodically, they beat him and prodded him with bayonets, kicked and spat at him and denied him any washing facilities.

On 20 August 1952, Kinne was made to stand to attention for seven hours. When he complained, the Chinese guard commander beat him with the butt of a sub machine gun. Ironically, this went off later and killed the guard commander. For this, Kinne was beaten senseless with belts and bayonets; stripped of his clothes and flung into a dank, rat-infested hole. Here they left him until 19 September. They took Kinne out regularly and beat him. On 16 September, they used pieces of planking and went on beating until he was unconscious.

On 16 October 1952, a Chinese military court tried Kinne for escaping and for being a reactionary, hostile to the Chinese. They sentenced him to twelve months' solitary confinement. When he complained about the sentence, they increased it to eighteen months. Kinne had complained of denial of medical attention, including that for a severe double hernia incurred earlier, in June 1952.

On 5 December 1952, they transferred Kinne to a special penal colony. His last sentence of solitary confinement came on Coronation Day, 2 June 1953, when he was punished for defying Chinese orders and wearing a rosette in celebration of the special day.

It seemed beyond belief that Kinne could have survived this catalogue of satanic treatment, but he was eventually exchanged at Panmunjon on 10 August 1953. As late as the previous two days, however, he had been threatened with non-repatriation for demanding an interview with the International Red Cross representative, visiting prisoner of war camps.

During the course of his periods of solitary confinement, the Chinese kept Kinne in no fewer than seven different places of imprisonment, including a security police gaol. The treatment he suffered was of the most extreme degradation and increasing brutality. Every possible physical and mental method was employed to try to break his spirit. He must have been fully aware, too, that every time he flaunted his opposition, and flouted his captors, he was risking his life. But he was determined to show his detestation of them and their methods. In fact, they threatened him with death several times. But Kinne was never intimidated by their barbarous nature and in this way won an immortal personal victory over them and their cruel creed.

John Axon, driver,
BRITISH RAIL

John Axon was driving a goods train between Buxton and Chapel-en-le-Frith on 11 February 1957. As he was about to halt the train prior to descending a steep gradient, the steam pipe fractured. Since this pipe fed the brake, the fracture wrecked the whole system of stopping the train. More than this, though, the break in the pipe resulted in scalding steam pouring into Axon's cab. The pressurized steam hissed out directly at his feet, causing third-degree burns.

John Axon had an immediate choice: to save himself or the runaway freight train. Aided by his fireman, he decided to try to halt the train before it ran down the steep slope. But with a failed brake system, they could not prevent it gathering speed down the decline. Axon called to the fireman: 'Jump clear.'

Then he added that the fireman should try to stop wagons by their individual brakes. But the train rolled on downhill, with boiling water now added to the steam in the driving cab. Axon probably knew that the train was beyond halting, but he stayed aboard, hoping he might be able somehow to control it. But it continued on, propelled by gravity, and collided forcibly with a second goods train, bound in a similar direction. The impact killed John Axon. He was still in his driving cab at the time.

Second Lieutenant Michael Paul Benner,
CORPS OF ROYAL ENGINEERS

Midsummer in the Austrian Alps. What could be more idyllic? A group of non-commissioned officers of the Royal Engineers were undergoing mountain training in these Alps. Second Lieutenant Benner was leading six NCOs up the 12,400-feet Grossglockner peak. By six o'clock on the evening of 1 July 1957, they had weathered a sudden storm and were struggling on their way to the summit.

Even at this time of year, they had limited hours left before darkness, so started their descent soon after unroping. Benner was in his rightful place, leading their route down a ridge. The earlier storm and the late hour combined to make the descent hazardous.

The NCO immediately following Benner slid down a steep, slippery angle. Benner was in no danger, but he at once relinquished his own foothold to catch the man. As he grasped the NCO with one of his hands, Benner struggled to stick his axe into some secure snow. The surface was unresponding as Benner refused to let go of the man's arm. He went on frantically in the frozen surface of snow, desperately seeking to stop the slide with either his ice axe or his feet. They were together now and it was too late for Benner to change his mind. In any case, it is certain that he would not have done so.

The two of them continued the lethal slide. Their silhouettes faded over the face of the Grossglockner. Second Lieutenant Benner sacrificed his own life trying to save one of the men in his charge.

Police Constable Henry William Stevens,
METROPOLITAN POLICE

Officers of police forces are always vulnerable to unexpected danger and so are probably prepared for it, if only unconsciously. Whether this was the case with Police Constable Stevens is not really known. On 29 March 1958, Stevens was in plain clothes while doing police radio car patrol in company with two other officers.

Over the car radio came a sudden message to hurry to a house in Bickley, Kent, where the police had heard of a break-in, or at least, a suspected one. They arrived at the house quietly. Stevens' two colleagues went to the front, while he took the rear. As he made his way round towards the back door, the form of a man fleetingly leapt an adjoining fence and headed for a nearby bridge over a railway line.

Stevens instantly started to chase him on foot. The policeman closed considerably towards the suspect, until only a matter of paces separated them. As Stevens increased his pace and ran directly at the man, the suspect suddenly swung round with a firearm and shot the constable in the mouth. The man ran on, but despite the terrible wound, Stevens actually staggered on and grabbed him.

They grappled together for a minute, before the man got away, minus his firearm, coat and hat. Losing blood copiously, Stevens tried to pursue the man, until his two police colleagues arrived to give him urgent medical aid. An ambulance summoned by radio hurried him to hospital.

The sequel to the story was that after a successful operation Stevens recovered fully. The criminal was caught and duly convicted and Henry Stevens rose to the rank of a chief inspector in the Metropolitan Police.

Chapter Ten

1960–1970

Raymond Tasman Donoghue,
TRAM CONDUCTOR

This accident happened at almost the most distant location of the British Commonwealth – Hobart, Tasmania. It was during a busy time of day on 29 April 1960 that one of the city's trams and an unspecified motor vehicle were in serious collision. The tram was on its normal route towards the Hobart suburb of Springfield when the accident occurred.

The cab housing the tram driver was totally concertinaed, the driver, Raymond Donoghue, was not killed but hurt and the tram began to career in reverse down a steep hill. Instead of acting to try to save his own life, Donoghue thought rapidly and shepherded the passengers to the back of the tram. At that stage, he still could have jumped from the tram or followed his passengers towards the back where it was safer.

Instead, Donoghue thought of the traffic volume and potential danger in the overall situation. He rang the tram's alarm as a warning to other vehicles, and also struggled to operate the handbrake installed for an emergency such as this. But the tram continued down the hill and reached the bottom, where it went into another stationary tram. Donoghue remained at his self-appointed position as the two trams collided, and he died. But there was no doubt at all that his actions saved other lives at the cost of his own.

Chief Petty Officer Jonathan Rogers,
ROYAL AUSTRALIAN NAVY

Welsh-born Jonathan Rogers earned a brief but moving tribute in the citation to his posthumous George Cross. Chief Petty Officer Rogers' ship, HMS *Voyager*, collided with another vessel on 10 February 1964. This is one of those rare risks for all mariners, but one that is always possible.

Before the *Voyager* sank, Rogers was responsible for saving the lives of many of his junior seamen. The experienced forty-three-year-old chief did his best to maintain the spirits of everyone in his charge. When it became apparent to him that no more could be saved, Rogers 'encouraged them to meet their death with dignity and honour'. From the moment of the collision, the actions of Rogers met the highest conceivable standards of the Royal Australian Navy.

An ironic postscript to this tragedy was that the location of the collision was off the Australian coast in an area known as Jervis Bay. This was, of course, the name of the immortal converted merchant liner which helped to save a convoy in the Second World War before being sunk by the German pocket battleship *Admiral Scheer*.

Michael Joseph Munnelly,
JOURNALIST

The particularly poignant dates of this incident were Christmas Eve and Christmas Day, 1964. The location was London, at Regent's Park Road. A gang of some fourteen drunken male teenagers were trying to gain entry to a flat in the road. When the occupier attempted to turn them away, they attacked him.

They then snatched bottles from a dairy on the opposite side of the road, smashed the flat's windows and went for the dairyman who was the occupant of the flat. The man had ventured from his flat into the road to try to stop them.

Thirty-nine-year-old journalist Michael Munnelly and two others who lived on the third storey of the house, went to the assistance of the dairyman. They managed to get hold of two of the youths, but another hit Munnelly over the head.

Some of the teenagers had gone off in a van but came back, presumably to pick up others. Munnelly's friend followed the van into another road, trying to make the youth at the wheel stop. After he got hold of a youth in the passenger seat, another kicked him into unconsciousness. Michael Munnelly ran to try to help his friend, but someone kicked him, too. Then he was stabbed in the stomach and died on Christmas Day.

Brian Spillett,
DETAIL FITTER

As a member of the 198th Parachute Regiment, Royal Horse Artillery Territorial Army, Brian Spillett could be said to be used to the occasional risk. But what happened to him on 9 January 1965 had nothing to do with the air. Before dawn, at about 5.30 a.m., fire broke out in a neighbouring house to his home in Waltham Cross. Brian heard shouting, looked out, saw the flames, pulled on a few clothes, and rushed into the road. Someone said to him: 'There's a man trapped inside.'

The fire was spreading by the second. Brian broke free from onlookers' efforts to restrain him, and headed into the fire. It must have been worse than he had thought, because he could not rescue the man. He himself was saved from the fire, but exactly one week afterwards the varied injuries inflicted by it proved irreversible and he died.

Wallace Arnold Oakes,
TRAIN DRIVER

Still in the days of steam trains, Wallace Arnold Oakes was the locomotive driver of a ten-coach passenger train. It was 5 June 1965 and while six or seven miles short of the famous junction of Crewe, the train was running normally at 60 mph. It was carrying many passengers.

148

Suddenly smoke swirled into the cab of the engine, with flames tonguing back from the engine's firebox. The fireman's clothes caught fire but, by prompt thinking, he managed to reach the steps of the cab and managed to extinguish the flames.

Wallace Oakes could have got out of his cab the instant that the original danger occurred. Instead, he put on the brakes of his engine, opened the blower and shut the regulator. He stayed with the locomotive while it slowed to an eventual halt. Oakes also did everything possible to minimize any danger from the blowback, and so avoided serious danger to his passengers. When the fireman went back to the cab, Oakes was not there but on the slope of the rail cutting in front of the engine. More than three-quarters of his body had been terribly burnt and though still alive, he died the following week. A locomotive was later named after him and he is also commemorated at Crewe, and at Nantwich, his birthplace.

Police Constable Anthony John Gledhill

Five men were in a car careering, against the traffic, down a one-way road. Police Constable Anthony Gledhill and another officer patrolling in their car were dispatched to catch the vehicle before it could cause serious harm. It was on 25 August 1966 in Deptford, south-east London, and the situation soon developed into a chase between the two cars, travelling up to 80 mph.

Over the course of this five-mile race, men within the law-breaking vehicle started shooting at the police car. Using a sawn-off shotgun and also a revolver, they aimed a total of fifteen shots at the two policemen trailing them. Then their car hurtled into a goods vehicle.

The men piled out of the car, whereupon the policemen, totally without weapons, chased them on foot and caught one of them. The policemen kept this gunman in their charge until back-up came to their assistance. All this time, Gledhill and the second police officer were suffering from injuries received in their confrontation with the gunmen. Fortunately they both recovered after treatment. But facing five criminals, who had already fired at them repeatedly, could easily have cost them their lives. Gledhill was recognized by the award of the George Cross.

Barbara Jane Harrison,
STEWARDESS, BRITISH OVERSEAS AIRWAYS CORPORATION

The time of take-off is always one of the most vulnerable in any flight. A Boeing 707 of British Overseas Airways Corporation left the runway at London's Heathrow Airport on 8 April 1968. Moments later, the airliner's No. 2 port engine suddenly flashed into fire and fell off. Flames continued to scorch into the gap remaining after the engine had gone, endangering the entire port wing.

Throughout the airliner, aircrew and cabin staff went into their emergency drill. The flight deck crew performed perfectly, effecting an emergency landing back on the tarmac at Heathrow. As the airliner braked, Stewardess Barbara Harrison and a steward had the duty of preparing the emergency escape for passengers at the back of the Boeing. Between them they inflated the necessary chute, which became twisted outside the fuselage. The steward clambered down to get it ready for use by the passengers but he had no means of boarding the aircraft again.

Barbara Harrison started to assist passengers to escape from the increasing state of emergency. Some leapt down in a frame of mind approaching desperation, while others had to be pressured into jumping. Barbara got many of them away safely, but then she and the remaining passengers were faced with a mixture of smoke, fire and electrical explosions. It was obvious that no more could escape via the tail emergency exit, so Barbara thought quickly and pointed passengers to a secondary way out.

She herself did not accompany them, as an elderly disabled passenger remained at the rear, unable to walk. Barbara struggled amid the increasing nightmare engulfing her. The disabled person was right at the rear of the seating accommodation, and Barbara tried with all her strength to succeed in a rescue attempt.

But the conditions in the cabin had become beyond bearing by that time and she lost consciousness. A little later, rescuers reached the bodies of Barbara and the disabled passenger, close to each other.

Chapter Eleven

1971–1977

Sergeant Michael Willetts,
3RD BATTALION, THE PARACHUTE REGIMENT

Belfast 1971: IRA terrorism had already been active for two years. It was an early summer evening, 25 May, when a terrorist got into the entrance hall of Springfield Road Police Station. Security, at that stage, had yet to reach the stricter levels of later years. The suitcase he was carrying had a visibly smoking fuse. The man deposited the case rapidly and departed with equal haste.

The occupants of the immediate area were police officers, as well as a man and woman with two children. It did not take long for the smoking fuse to alert the policemen, who began to get people away from the hall.

Sergeant Willetts, of the Parachute Regiment, was in an adjacent area. As soon as the alarm reached him, he dispatched another non-commissioned officer upstairs to alert staff there. Willetts then hurried to hold an outer door open to enable all those inside to hurry away from the suitcase. This was all happening in seconds now. Willetts stayed in the doorway and shielded others from any immediate blast.

At that moment the bomb in the case went off, with the added power associated with an explosion in a confined interior. The adults and children he had been shielding were saved from most

152

of the effects by the physical bulk of Sergeant Willetts. But, tragically, he took its main eruptive thrust and was killed. A forerunner of Northern Ireland's too many fatalities.

Errol John Emanuel,
DISTRICT COMMISSIONER, PAPUA

On the other side of the globe from Britain, Errol Emanuel became District Commissioner for the East New Britain area, Papua, in March 1971, continuing nearly two years of previous work in trying to harmonize hostile local groups. Now as District Commissioner, Emanuel travelled alone to various villages. His aim in going alone was to inspire the trust of all local leaders and to persuade them towards pacific ways rather than violence. Danger was always present on these frequent visits, but by his solitary sorties he knew that none of his colleagues or the police could be exposed to risks.

19 August 1971: Emanuel was acting in his role of peacemaker in the midst of a confrontation among hostile groups. There had actually been death threats to Emanuel just before this date, and some people he met were daubed with war paint. These were warning signs, but he chose to ignore them and continue with his duties. He could have invoked police protection, but again he preferred not to risk their lives.

Some so-called 'dissidents' invited him to accompany them, in the hope that he might be able to intercede in a dangerous disturbance and so stop the possibility of an internecine clash. However, although Emanuel had taken many such chances during his long period in Papua, this would be his last gamble. One group set upon him and slew him. So died Errol Emanuel, peacemaker.

Superintendent Gerald Irving Richardson,
LANCASHIRE CONSTABULARY
Police Constable Carl Walker,
LANCASHIRE CONSTABULARY

Armed criminals raided a Blackpool jeweller's shop on 23 August 1971. After the alarm had been raised, police cars chased the raiders. By dogged defiance, the unarmed police kept close to the raiders and Police Constable Walker temporarily cut off the criminals in a cul-de-sac by driving his police Panda car across the path of the parked getaway vehicle.

The raiders reversed at speed, striking the side of the police car. Walker was shocked by the impact, but set off on foot after a trio of armed men. One of them fired at him from short range, injuring his groin.

Meanwhile, Superintendent Richardson was chasing another of the robbers and attempting to make him forfeit his firearm. The man turned, aimed the gun and shot the defenceless Superintendent in the stomach. Robbing a jeweller's shop was bad enough, carrying guns was even worse, but most terrible of all was merciless murder of a senior policeman, or any policeman. Although rushed to hospital, Superintendent Richardson died later that same day. In due course, Carl Walker became a police inspector.

Major Stephen George Styles,
ROYAL ARMY ORDNANCE CORPS

It was still comparatively early times in the troubles of Northern Ireland. Major Styles was serving there, overseeing Royal Army Ordnance Corps teams charged with disposing of explosive concoctions created by terrorists.

It was 20 October 1971 when Styles faced an unknown device. It was found in a phone booth at Belfast's famous Europa Hotel. Evacuation drill was followed, then Styles assumed control of neutralizing the device before it was taken away for disposal.

22 October now and another bomb brought Styles to the

Europa again. This one had a booby trap in its circuitry, meant to prevent anyone dismantling it. Styles began a concentrated period of neutralizing the thirty-pound bomb. This went on for nine hours before he had completed his tiring and potentially lethal duty.

By solving the circuitry of the bomb, he was able to safeguard the lives of future colleagues who might be called on to tackle a similar weapon.

James Kennedy,
SECURITY OFFICER, BRITISH RAIL ENGINEERING

Just four days before Christmas 1973, seven men planned a payroll robbery at the British Rail Engineering Works in Glasgow. Security guards were in the process of distributing pre holiday cash from a central block to the large organization's usual wages points. This was being done under cover of darkness before the start of the working day.

Half-a-dozen heavily armed robbers suddenly appeared and attacked the security guards who were transferring this money. Using a sawn-off shotgun, one of the six hit and wounded two of the guards, though not seriously. Then the six men hurried off, heading for the front way out of the whole complex.

The duty security officer at this main gate was James Kennedy, who heard the shots clearly over the night air. He must, therefore, have been aware that one or more of the men had a gun, but he placed himself squarely in the main gateway to try to stop the robbers making a getaway. Kennedy floored one robber, but others rounded on him with their gun barrels, struck him several times on the head and stunned him, causing two deep skull wounds.

Yet another of the robbers drove their escape van into position for the rest to board. Kennedy, although still stunned and in a state of grave shock, came to sufficiently to try to stop the getaway. As he moved in the direction of one of the van doors, the robber in the passenger seat nearest to it, loosed off two shots which killed him. It was only later that the severity of his skull wounds came to light.

If it is possible to add an appropriate denouncement to this terrible incident, it was the capture, conviction, and sentencing of all the robbers connected with this merciless murder of an unarmed security officer, who was protecting the Christmas wages of the men employed at the British Rail Engineering Works.

Sergeant Murray Ken Hudson,
ROYAL NEW ZEALAND INFANTRY REGIMENT

No one born in New Zealand had ever been awarded the George Cross before Sergeant Hudson. Nor had anyone won it as a result of an incident actually in that country. The irony of this case was that Hudson was a long-experienced soldier with previous service overseas in Malaya, Borneo and Vietnam, yet the George Cross incident occurred at a military camp in his home country.

As had happened elsewhere in the past, this accident involved hand grenades. It was 13 February 1974 when Hudson was in charge of throwing practice with these dangerous weapons. The non-commissioned officer in his particular bay somehow armed a grenade to be thrown. Hudson saw this at once and shouted to him: 'Throw it.'

For some reason, the man seemed to do nothing.

The total time before the grenade would be due to fire was a mere four seconds. Hudson tried to help the soldier toss the weapon beyond the protective parapet. The grenade rose towards it, but before it could sail over, the full force of its live filling exploded and both the sergeant and NCO were killed. Hudson had acted selflessly and nearly managed to avert the tragedy, but the four-second fuse was too brief. The amazing thing about the whole tragedy was how much Hudson actually did in so short a time.

Inspector James Wallace Beaton,
METROPOLITAN POLICE (ROYAL BODYGUARD)

The next GC award was highly unusual – for helping to foil a royal kidnap. In 1974, a thirty-one-year-old Scotsman, Inspector James Beaton was serving as 'personal police officer' to HRH Princess Anne; in other words, her bodyguard. Beaton did not know it then, but on one day that year he would be called on to act in his literal capacity of bodyguard.

At about eight o'clock in the evening of 20 March, Princess Anne and her husband at that time, Captain Mark Phillips, were heading back to Buckingham Palace from one of their official engagements. Their car was being driven by Mr Callender and they were accompanied by a lady-in-waiting and Inspector Beaton.

As the vehicle neared the junction of The Mall with Marlborough Road, a white car suddenly swung across in front of it. Mr Callender braked instinctively and the royal car stopped. The driver of the other vehicle left his car, and Beaton at once got out of his front passenger seat to approach the man. As he did so, the man suddenly raised a revolver, aimed at Beaton, and fired it. The shot wounded the bodyguard in his shoulder.

Despite his wound, Beaton drew his own protective pistol and fired at the man. The shot missed, however, and before Beaton could fire again his gun jammed. As Beaton moved to the nearside of the royal car to try to clear the blockage, the gunman called to him; 'Drop the gun or I'll shoot Princess Anne.'

The inspector had no alternative but to place his pistol on the ground. The gunman then tried to force open the rear offside door of the car, demanding that Princess Anne should get out and go with him. She and Captain Phillips were struggling to keep their door shut.

Meanwhile, the lady-in-waiting was able to get out by the rear nearside door, and Beaton scrambled in the same way. He at once leant across to shield Princess Anne with his body. Captain Phillips managed to close the door. Beaton saw that the man was about to fire into the back of the royal car, so put up his hand to the window in the line of fire to intercept the impact of any bullet.

157

The gunman fired, the car window shattered and Beaton was hit in the right hand by a combination of the bullet and the broken glass.

Despite his injuries, Beaton asked Captain Phillips to release his grip on the door, so that the bodyguard could kick it open and throw the gunman off balance. But before he could do so, the man himself opened the car door, fired again at Beaton, and wounded him, this time in the stomach. The inspector fell from the door and collapsed unconscious at the gunman's feet.

This was the end of Inspector Beaton's gallant part in the attempted kidnap, but far from the end of the episode as a whole.

Meanwhile, the royal driver Mr Callender had tried to get out of the car, but the gunman put a pistol to his head and told him not to move. Yet as soon as he could, Callender did get out and actually grabbed the man's arm. Although the gunman threatened to shoot him, Callender clung to the man's arm until he was shot in the chest.

Next on the scene came Mr McConnell, who heard the shots as he was in a taxi along The Mall. He got out, ran back to the scene and found the gunman shouting at all the occupants of the royal car. McConnell tried to reason with the gunman, asking him to hand over the weapon. As McConnell approached, the gunman fired and hit him in the chest. McConnell staggered away and collapsed.

Constable Hills then arrived from nearby St James's Palace. The gunman spun round and shot Hills, also in the stomach. Although staggering with the pain, the constable managed to send a personal radio message to Cannon Row Police Station calling for urgent help. By this time, he felt very faint and was assisted to the roadside, where be collapsed from his wound.

By this time, still others had entered the scene. Mr Martin was driving along The Mall when he saw the situation. He drove his car in front of the gunman's vehicle to prevent any possible escape. Martin hurried across to the royal car, but the gunman pushed a revolver in in his ribs. This was at the time the gunman had shot Constable Hills, and it was Martin who helped him to the roadside.

Next arrived Mr Russell, who had also been driving along The

Mall. By then, the gunman had shot Hills and was holding Princess Anne by the forearm. Russell ran up and punched him on the back of his head. The gunman at once turned and fired at him but fortunately missed.

The gunman was still trying to drag Princess Anne with one hand while pointing his gun at her with the other and threatening to shoot if she refused to come. While maintaining her refusal, the Princess managed to delay the gunman and distract him by actually talking to him. Captain Phillips kept his arm firmly round her waist and continued trying to pull her back into the car. The action was now nearing its climax.

Princess Anne broke free from the gunman and tried to leave the car by the nearside door. Russell ran round to the other side, too and the gunman came up behind him in a final effort to reach the Princess. Captain Phillips pulled her back into the car and Russell punched the man in the face. Constable Hills' radio call had been heard by this time and other police officers began to reach the scene. At this stage, the gunman ran off.

Constable Edmonds was one of the first officers on the scene. Edmonds saw the man running away, with the gun still in his hand. The constable shouted at him to stop, but he continued to run and point the weapon at the officer. Edmonds charged the man and knocked him to the ground. Other officers then arrived and disarmed the gunman.

The wounded men were all rushed to hospital, where bullets were successfully removed from Inspector Beaton, Mr Callender and Mr McConnell. Constable Hills received treatment for his wound, though no immediate attempt was made to remove a bullet from his liver. All the men involved revealed great gallantry and the kidnap plan was foiled. Due recognition was accorded to all those involved. Inspector James Beaton was awarded the George Cross and went on later to become a Chief Superintendent in the Metropolitan Police.

Captain Roger Philip Goad,
EXPLOSIVES OFFICER, METROPOLITAN POLICE

29 August 1975: two men were the participants in this episode – one gallant, the other evil. A terrorist deposited a bomb in the doorway of a London shop. Its location was notified to a national paper. Captain Roger Goad went to deal with it, as an explosives officer in the Metropolitan Police.

Before his arrival, the police had discovered a plastic bag in the place reported. Close investigation revealed a watch was connected to the contents, which seemed to confirm that it was a bomb. After the area had been evacuated, the Police brought Goad up to date with all the information they had been able to find, short of actually touching or tackling the suspect bag.

Goad went into the doorway of the shop by himself, to minimize possible casualties. Onlookers, from a distance, detected him reach the bomb, bend over it, and presumably start the hazardous process of trying to dismantle it.

The detonation wrecked the doorway, shattered surrounding glass, and killed Captain Goad.

John Clements,
SCHOOLMASTER

Accidents appear doubly tragic when they happen on holiday and, especially so, when children are involved. The location of this disaster was the north Italian ski resort of Sappada. Thirty-seven children and six adults from Welwyn Garden City's Sherrardswood School were staying at a hotel at Sappada on the night of 11–12 April 1976. Twenty-two-year-old John Clements was one of the schoolmasters in the group.

4 a.m.: the smell of smoke aroused Clements and several others. Their first thought was for the children, some of whom were escorted safely through thickening smoke. Clements clambered from the third floor down to the second, via the projecting balconies, to the rooms. All the while, the fire was intensifying.

Clements knew that there were still children on the first floor unaccounted for, so proceeded by the external balconies down to that level. He got them into groups, tied sheets together firmly and assisted them to ground level by this classic emergency means. He also helped to keep a degree of calmness among them. As soon as he was satisfied that this batch had escaped, Clements returned into the hotel interior.

The fire had taken drastic hold by then, but he continued to manhandle people to places of safety. There were still some trapped by fumes or fire, and Clements himself eventually succumbed to the quantity of smoke he had, inevitably, inhaled. He collapsed and died, having been solely responsible for the salvation of many of the survivors of this fateful night.

Constable Michael Kenneth Pratt,
VICTORIA POLICE, MELBOURNE, AUSTRALIA

Coincidences can occur at any time. They are or may be the result of one or more conscious or unconscious decisions made daily in all our lives. This was certainly so in the case of twenty-one-year-old Constable Michael Pratt in the Victorian capital of Melbourne.

He was off duty in his home town during the morning of 4 June 1976. Two events combined to create the coincidence that affected his life on that day. The first was that he was driving his car in the Clifton Hill area of the city and passed a bank. The second event was the real coincidence in timing. Pratt actually saw three men, wearing masks, go into the bank with guns.

Instinctively, Pratt swung his car round, pressed his horn, and drove across the pavement. At this angle he had cut off the entrance – and exit – of the bank. Police help was summoned simultaneously. As he was not on duty, Pratt carried no weapon. The bank robbers were caught unawares by his action with the car and one of them, brandishing a gun, told the constable to drive off. Pratt's response was to immobilize his car rapidly by pulling out its ignition key. He also snatched up a car jack handle.

The robbers decided they had better try to get away, but Pratt got hold of one man and hit him into unconsciousness. Another robber came out of the bank and aimed, as if to fire at the constable, from pointblank range.

The original man came to at that stage, so Pratt had to concentrate again on trying to get him into custody. A shot suddenly sounded and Pratt fell. Although badly injured by the bullet, fortunately he survived the ordeal to receive the George Cross for facing three armed bank robbers with 'complete disregard for his own safety'.

Captain Robert Laurence Nairac,
GRENADIER GUARDS

Some men stand out from others. Twenty-eight-year-old Captain Robert Nairac was definitely one of these. He served no fewer than four tours of duty in trouble-torn Northern Ireland, where his demeanour, both physical and mental, became an inspiration to other soldiers. His fourth tour was destined to be his last. The bare brief of Nairac's role was as liaison officer associated with surveillance. He was based at the headquarters of 3 Infantry Brigade, Grenadier Guards.

Seven or more men captured him from a South Armagh village over a mid-May night in 1977. Nairac fought fiercely, but was removed into the nearby Irish Republic. The Captain possessed intelligence that could, and probably would, have endangered lives and plans. His abductors tortured him to try to get at these names and future intentions.

Not only did Nairac resist their savagery, but over the ensuing hours he even made a number of efforts to get away from captivity. He must have known his probable fate even before a provisional IRA gunman was brought to the scene. Somewhere in Ireland on 15 May 1977, this man murdered Captain Robert Nairac. His body was never found.

Chapter Twelve

1989–2009

Warrant Officer Barry Johnson,
ROYAL ARMY ORDNANCE CORPS

It is no coincidence that a number of men of the Royal Army Ordnance Corps feature in the roll of George Cross winners.

One such man was Warrant Officer Barry Johnson.

The familiar setting for such an emergeney was Northern Ireland. The date: 7 October 1989 and the location Londonderry. An abandoned and unidentified van had been spotted beside a hospital. In the vehicle was a six-tube mortar bomb and the van was parked in the middle of a residential estate in Waterside, Londonderry.

Johnson was assigned to investigate the report and his first consideration had to be for the people living within range, together with the patients of the adjoining hospital. The normal drill would have been to tackle the suspect device by remote-controlled equipment long developed for the job. Here, however, he started to extract the mortars from the six tubes and deal with them by his own hand. Aided by an assistant, the Warrant Officer lifted the firing tubes out of the van with infinite care and put them down equally meticulously.

Things could have become still more dangerous from then on, so Johnson told his junior to withdraw to cover. He aimed the firing tubes in such a direction that if they exploded there would be no civilian casualties. It was a cold, dark, autumnal night and had begun to rain. Combating these obstacles and the resultant slippery surfaces, Johnson withdrew each bomb and rendered it safe. He had dismantled five of the six bombs when the last bomb went off.

His face, legs and, most serious of all, his eyes were all damaged. Fragments from the weapon temporarily blinded him – and the main blast blew him right over the road. Johnson was in pain from all these injuries, but he insisted on ensuring that his helper was in possession of enough facts to enable him to finish the assignment. Warrant Officer Barry Johnson survived the ordeal.

Sergeant Stewart Graeme Guthrie,
NEW ZEALAND POLICE

A nightmare massacre of a dozen people marked the start of these events. It was a late spring dusk, 13 November 1990, in New Zealand. At the normally peaceful seaside resort of Aramoana, outside Dunedin, a young gunman suddenly went berserk shooting and killing twelve people and injuring as many again.

A message was rushed through to the nearest police station, where Sergeant Guthrie was the only officer present. By a description of the man and the catastrophic casualties he had caused, Guthrie seemed to recognize his identity.

The sergeant hurried to the scene and, together with a police constable, he went to the gunman's home. The constable took the front approach; the sergeant, the rear. Both policemen were armed, while three more colleagues augmented them a little later forming a ring around the property.

The police control centre was aware that Guthrie hoped to keep the gunman in the house. The next move actually came from the man, who broke some windows and tossed out an incendiary device. Then he came outside and aimed a gun towards one of the policemen. But he thought better of it and rapidly returned inside.

Sergeant Guthrie was under cover behind a second dwelling, adjacent to that of the gunman. It was dark now, when the gunman appeared out of nowhere. Guthrie issued an instant

164

verbal challenge to him and let off a warning round as a deterrent to further action. But this was utterly of no avail. The gunman aimed a whole succession of shots towards Guthrie, murdering him on the spot.

When daylight returned to the scene, the gunman was embroiled with the police and fatally fired on by them.

Royal Ulster Constabulary

The following was the official George Cross citation issued by Buckingham Palace on 23 November 1999.

> For the past 30 years, the Royal Ulster Constabulary has been the bulwark against, and the main target of, a sustained and brutal terrorism campaign. The Force has suffered heavily in protecting both sides of the community from danger – 302 officers have been killed in the line of duty and thousands more have been injured, many seriously. Many officers have been ostracised by their own community and others have been forced to leave their homes in the face of threats to them and their families.
>
> As Northern Ireland reached a turning point in its political development this award is made to recognise the collective courage and dedication to duty of all of those who have served in the Royal Ulster Constabulary and who have accepted the danger and stress this has brought to them and their families.

In its sixty-eight-year history from 1922 to 1990, the Royal Ulster constabulary suffered a total of 302 officers killed and more than 8,300 injured, some of them very seriously. During those years, the attacks on police stations exceeded 3,300. In November 2001, the Royal Ulster Constabulary became the Police Service of Northern Ireland.

The award of the George Cross was made especially to honour those officers who gave their lives. The following are just a few of them, representing the many:

Reserve Constables William Finlay and James Ferguson were murdered by the IRA as they patrolled on foot. Around nine shots were fired at the officers, hitting them in the necks and shoulders.

Constable Michael Todd was shot dead as he and colleagues approached a house in which armed terrorists were hiding.

Inspector James Hazlett was shot by the IRA in the garden of his own home as he walked his dog.

Inspector Dave Ead was shot by the IRA while on patrol. Two gunmen came up behind Inspector Ead and opened fire, hitting him in the baek.

Constables Gary Meyer and Harold John Beckett were shot dead from behind by IRA gunmen as they walked on duty.

Constable Sam Todd was a dog-handler shot dead by the IRA. He and a colleague were sitting in an unmarked van when gunmen opened fire from close range. The other officer was badly wounded but survived.

The George Cross was actually presented to the Royal Ulster Constabulary at Hillsborough Castle, Belfast, on 12 April 2000 by HM Queen Elizabeth II. At this time, one officer was selected especially as symbolizing the spirit of all those who served – past and present. His experience sums up the courage of the Constabulary. His name: Constable Paul Slaine. This is what happened to him:

Paul Slaine joined the Royal Ulster Constabulary from university in May 1988. He was posted to Newry in September of that year.

Just over three years later, at 11.40 pm, on Friday, 27th March 1992, a remote-controlled mortar was fired by Provisional IRA terrorists at a mobile patrol in the town's Merchant's Quay. Thirty-four-year-old Constable Colleen McMurray, a police officer with fifteen years' service, died in hospital a short time later.

Paul Slaine had both his legs blown off in the attack and sustained other injuries.

In a statement to a Belfast newsroom, the terrorists said: 'The device . . . scored a direct hit and volunteers observed that the RUC Sierra car and its crew were completely devastated.'

Whilst Paul was recovering from his horrific injuries, his wife, Allison, and their children were subjected to intimidation and had to be rehoused.

Paul's strength of will and determination enabled him to be presented to Diana, Princess of Wales, at a Hillsborough garden party three months later, on 30th June. He returned to work in November 1993 in the field of information technology.

Paul Slaine continues to be a serving RUC officer.

– Royal Ulster Constabulary, April 2000.

Trooper Christopher Finney, The Blues and Royals of The Household Cavalry Regiment

Eighteen-year-old Trooper Christopher Finney is the youngest British serviceman to be awarded tbe George Cross and also the most recent. The date of the deed: 28 March 2003. The place: north of Basra, Iraq.

Operation Telic was the codename applied to the hostilities in Iraq. During the afternoon of 28 March, Trooper Finney was patrolling with 2 Troop of D Squadron, The Blues and Royals of the Household Cavalry Regiment. Their area was up the west side of Route Spear, running alongside the Shatt-Al-Arab waterway, north of Basra.

They had been briefed to locate and destroy the Iraqi 6th Armoured Division, greatly superior in force to themselves. A Scimitar armoured reconnaissance vehicle was being driven by Finney, followed by a second, when two American A10 aircraft loomed up overhead and started loosing cannons at them on Route Spear. The opening burst of depleted uraninm shells came from two of the deadliest close-attack aircraft of the United States Air Force.

Finney said: 'I saw the A10. It wasn't very high up. I could see everything, even the pilot. We set off red smoke to warn them we were friendly.'

Both Scimitars caught fire, with ammunition going off inside their respective turrets. This first attacking run of 'friendly fire' caused four of Finney's colleagues to be wounded. Lance Corporal Tudbole, the gunner of his vehicle, was not only injured but trapped, too. Finney clambered on top of the burning Scimitar, somehow dragging his comrade out of it, deposited him in a safer place and began to bandage the man's wounds.

This first run by the two A10s left the entire immediate area shrouded by smoke. Through the chaos, Finney groped his way back to the Scimitar and radioed his headquarters with the news of the attack.

With the two Scimitars immobilized, a Royal Engineers Spartan vehicle advanced to aid the casualties. As it approached the scene, the crew could see Finney carrying the injured Lance Corporal Al Tudbole towards them. But at that instant, the A10s had veered round and launched a second strike. This attacking run hit Finney in his lower back and legs, while wounding Tudbole afresh, this time in the head.

Despite his own injuries, Finney got Tudbole back to the Spartan and inside it. But Finney did not stay there. He then tried to climb on to the rear of the second Scimitar to rescue the driver Lance Corporal of Horse, Matty Hull. However, the searing smoke and exploding ammunition forced him back. Lance Corporal Hull died. Lance Corporal Tudbole recovered after prolonged treatment.

Trooper Christopher Finney's citation said:

> He displayed clear-headed courage and devotion to his comrades which was out of all proportion to his age and experience. Acting with complete disregard for his own safety even when wounded, his bravery was of the highest order.

Or as one of his colleagues put it: 'Finney helped people out of the wagon. He was the man who was amazing.'

Captain Peter Norton, Royal Logistic Corps

This was the second George Cross to be awarded for service in Iraq. Forty-three-year-old Peter Norton had been in bomb disposal for twenty years at the time of his heroic action. As an ammunition technical officer serving on the outskirts of Baghdad, he showed the most conspicuous courage in circumstances of extreme danger. He was second in command of a US/British explosives unit under the title US Combined Explosives Exploitation Cell. This unit had been in the forefront of operations against explosive devices improvised by the insurgents.

At 19.17 hours on 24 July 2005, a three-vehicle patrol from the US Georgia National Guard sustained a massive improvised explosive device (IED) in the Al Bayaa district near Baghdad, resulting in the utter destruction of a Humvee patrol vehicle and the deaths of four US personnel. In view of the significance of this horrific attack, a team commanded by Captain Norton received orders to hurry to the scene.

On Norton's arrival, the aftermath of the blast presented a picture of confusion and carnage. He ordered his men of the coalition forces to stay in safety, while he went forward to investigate. He was told that a possible remote command wire had been spotted in the vicinity of the explosion site. The insurgents had used such secondary follow-up devices in this dangerous region of Iraq.

As Norton advanced cautiously, another explosion did, in fact, shatter the air – and himself. He had trodden on a victim-operated device that initiated instantaneous and traumatic amputation of his left leg at the knee, as well as blast and fragmentation wounds to his other leg, both arms, and his lower abdomen. Later he actually recalled the moment of being flung in the air.

When his team instinctively rushed forward to help him, Norton remained conscious and lucid. But before letting them give him first aid, he indicated to the team where the safe area lay. Despite his grievous injuries, Captain Norton insisted on ignoring these and remained in command of the situation during the follow-up activities.

In the words of the official account, Norton regarded the safety

169

of his men as paramount, before permitting them to give him life-saving aid. A little later another device was found only ten yards away and rendered safe the next day. Norton's prescience and clear orders prevented any further loss of life and his heroism saved at least seven lives. His actions encapsulated the essence of that simple phrase inscribed on the George Cross, 'For Gallantry'.

Corporal Mark William Wright, The 3rd Battalion, The Parachute Regiment

Mark Wright was awarded the George Cross for his outstanding bravery on 6 September 2006 in Afghanistan. He entered a mine-field in an extraordinary attempt to save the lives of critically-injured soldiers. Sadly, he lost his life in this heroic effort.

Mark was deployed to Helmand Province as a mortar fire controller in May 2006, operating across this dangerous province. He was vital in controlling mortar fire for a variety of sub units. Throughout the tour, Wright was continuously in the field conducting high-intensity operations right until his death.

From July 2006, a fire support group of 3rd Battalion, The Parachute Regiment held a high ridge in the northern centre of Helmand Province, near the Kajaki Dam. On 6 September the leader of a sniper group was tasked with engaging Taliban fighters operating on the main highway. The patrol leader was heading down the steep slope when he initiated a mine and sustained severe injuries.

Seeing the mine-strike from higher up, Mark Wright gathered a group of men and rushed down the slope to assist. Realising that the casualty was likely to die before full mine clearance could be effected, Wright led his men into the minefield. Taking decisive command, Wright directed medical orderlies to the injured soldier; ordered all unnecessary soldiers to safety and then began organising the evacuation of casualties. He called for a helicopter and ordered a route to be cleared through the mine-field to a landing site. Unfortunately, the leader of the group on this task stepped on another mine and suffered a traumatic amputation.

Once more at enormous risk, Corporal Wright immediately hurried to this new casualty and began rendering life-saving help until a medical orderly could take over the task. Calmly, Wright ordered all non-essential personnel to stay out of the minefield. Wright himself continued to move around and control the situation. He sent accurate reports to his headquarters and ensured the delivery of additional medical items.

Shortly afterwards, a helicopter landed nearby, but as Wright stood up he initiated a third mine which wounded him seriously together with one of the orderlies. The remaining medical orderly began treating Wright but was himself injured by another mine blast. This caused further injuries to Corporal Wright and others.

Seven casualties were then still in the lethal minefield, three of whom had lost limbs. Despite this horrific situation and the serious injuries he had sustained himself, Wright continued to control the incident, shouting encouragement and maintaining morale among the wounded men. Tragically, Corporal Wright died of his wounds in the rescue helicopter. His George Cross citation quotes his supreme courage, outstanding leadership, greatest gallantry and disregard for his own safety in striving to save others.

Lance Corporal Matthew Croucher, Royal Marine Reservist

Sometimes a citation for the George Cross needs the minimum modification for the maximum effect. The award to Matthew Croucher is one such case.

Throughout December 2007 and January 2008 in Afghanistan, a forward operating base south of Sangin had been targeted relentlessly by an enemy seeking to inflict injury and death on Coalition Forces. The Taliban had been deploying complex improvised explosive devices (IEDs) in this area with devastating success. Troops compelled to move around here ran high risks, whether operating on foot or in vehicles. Yet 40 Commando

Reconnaissance Force was determined to regain the initiative.

Lance Corporal Croucher was in Helmand Province as a reconnaissance operator in part of 40 Commando Group. On 9 February 2008 they received orders to reconnoitre a compound where it was suspected that Taliban fighters were manufacturing IEDs.

Matthew Croucher's section was deployed on this dangerous job. Utilising night vision devices and under constant threat from explosive sources or enemy ambush, they managed to negotiate the varied terrain between their base and the suspect compound. Here they established an over-watch position to observe any enemy activity.

The decision was then made to send in a small four-man team – including Matthew Croucher – to conduct a high-risk "close target reconnaissance." This plan involved the quartet actually entering the enemy compound. This they accomplished without incident. After about half an hour, they had identified numerous items that could be used for bomb making. At this stage the team commander gave the order for them to withdraw to a rendezvous point with the rest of the Commando Force.

Lance Corporal Croucher was at the head of the quartet as they commenced withdrawal. Five metres behind him, the team commander and another Marine were fully exposed in the open, with the fourth man a short way behind them.

As they moved silently through the compound and the night, Croucher felt a trip-wire go tight against his legs just below the knees. This was connected to a grenade positioned to kill or maim intruders to the compound. Matthew then heard the fly-off lever eject. The armed grenade fell onto the ground behind him. Instantly realising what had happened, Croucher made a crucial and incredibly rapid assessment. With remarkable clarity and composure, he shouted the word 'Grenade' and then 'Tripwire'. He said later, 'I was just gritting my teeth waiting for the explosion and I had that deep gut feeling of "This is going to hurt . . . . I'm in serious trouble now."'

In a literally split-second decision, rather than seek cover or protection for himself, he tried to shield the others from the inevitable explosion. In an act of extreme courage, Croucher threw himself on top of the grenade, pinning it between his ruck-sack and the ground. The rear man had time to step back around the corner of a building, but the other three remained exposed and within lethal range of the grenade.

The grenade went off.

As it detonated, its blast effect was absorbed by Croucher. Most of the fragmentation was contained under his body. Miraculously his equipment and protective clothing stopped any deadly shards from hitting his body. He suffered only minor injury and disori-entation. But his rucksack was ripped from his back and utterly obliterated. Fragments from the grenade pitted his body armour and helmet. A large battery being carried in the side pouch of the rucksack also exploded and burnt like a flare. The only other injury was a slight wound to the team commander's face.

That the others escaped unscathed, was certainly due to Croucher's selfless action. He had prevented death or injury to at least half the members of the small team. Immediately after the explosion they managed to manoeuvre back to their rendezvous location. Croucher refused to be evacuated and, along with his other team members, engaged and neutralised one Taliban fighter. At the time of writing, the Afghanistan war continues . . .

Appendix

Winners of other awards eligible for conversion to the George Cross.

Initials after names denote awards as follows:-

EGM	Empire Gallantry Medal
AM	Albert Medal
EM	Edward Medal

Abbott, Edmund AM
Adamson, George EGM
Ali Bey, Yusuf EGM
Allport, Ernest, EM
Anderson, Walter EGM
Armytage, Reginald AM
Ashburnham, Doreen AM
Atkinson, Thomas EGM
Bain-Smith, George AM
Baldev Singh EGM
Barkat Singh EGM
Barraclough, Arnold EGM
Baster, Norman EM
Baxter, William EM
Beaman, George EM
Bell, John EGM
Blackburn, Richard EGM

Abbott, George AM
Alder, Thomas EGM
Allen, Florence AM
Anderson, Frederick EGM
Andrews, Wallace EGM
Arnold, Walter EGM
Ashraf-un-Nisa EGM
Bagot, Arthur AM
Baker, John EM
Baldwin, Wilson EM
Barnett, William EGM
Barwari, Rajah of EGM
Bastian, Gordon AM
Bayley, Clive EGM
Beattie, John EGM
Bhim Singh Yadava EGM
Blackburn, Sydney EM

174

Blogg, Henry **EGM**
Booker, David **EM**
Brett, Douglas **EGM**
Brown, David **EM**
Brown, Richard **AM**
Buckle, Henry **AM**
Burton, Herbert **EGM**
Button, William **EGM**
Cannon, Horace **AM**
Chalmers, Robert **EGM**
Charlton, John **EM**
Child, Frederick **EGM**
Clarke, Azariah **EM**
Close, Gerald **EGM**
Cowley, John **AM**
Crosby, Bertram **FM**
Darker, Richard **EM**
Day, Harry **AM**
Dixon, John **EM**
d'Souza, Baptist **EGM**
Edwards, Arthur **EM**
Elston, Ernest **EGM**
Fairclough, John **AM**
Farrow, Kenneth **AM**
Feetham, Christopher **AM**
Fleming, William **EGM**
Flintoff, Henry Harwood **EM**
Fraser, Harriet **AM**
Ghulam Mohi-ud-Din **EGM**
Gibbs, Stanley **AM**
Golandaz, Abdus **EGM**
Graveley, Reginald **EGM**
Haller, Fred **EM**
Harris, Charles **EM**
Harwood, Harrie **AM**
Hawkins, Eynon **AM**
Hemeida, El Amin **EGM**
Henshaw, George **EGM**

Bogdanovich, Theodore **EGM**
Booker, Samuel **EM**
Brooks, Arthur **EGM**
Brown, John **EM**
Bryson, Oliver **AM**
Burke, James **EGM**
Butson, Arthur **AM**
Campion, Michael **EGM**
Chalmers, Jack **AM**
Chant, Frederick **EGM**
Charrington, Harold **EGM**
Clark, Joseph **EGM**
Cleall, Walter **AM**
Cobham, Anthony **EGM**
Craig, Bert **EM**
Crossley, Edwin **EGM**
Davis, Thomas **AM**
Deedes, Richard **EGM**
Douglas, Robert **EGM**
Duffin, Charles **EGM**
Ellis, Bernard **AM**
Evans, David **AM**
Farr, John **EGM**
Fattah, Rashid **EGM**
Fisher, Bernard **EM**
Fletcher, Donald **EM**
Ford, Albert **AM**
Frost, Ernest **EGM**
Gibbons , John **AM**
Goad, William **AM**
Gough, John **EM**
Gregson, John **AM**
Hand, William **EGM**
Harrison, George **EGM**
Havercroft, Percy **EM**
Hay, David **AM**
Henderson, Herbert **EGM**
Heslop, George **EM**

175

Hodge, Alexander **EGM**
Hulme, Thomas **EM**
Hutchinson, John **EM**
Idris, Taha **EGM**
Jamieson, William **EGM**
Jolly, Richard **EGM**
Kavanaugh, Robert **AM**
Kent, Ernest **EM**
Khalifa, Muhammad **EGM**
Knowlton, Richard **AM**
Little, Robert **EM**
Locke, George **EM**
Lowe, Alfred **AM**
Lynch, Joseph **AM**
Maltby, Reginald **EGM**
March, Frederick **EGM**
Maxwell-Hyslop, Alexander **AM**
McAloney, William **AM**
McCabe, John **EGM**
McCarthy, **AM**
McCormack, Thomas **AM**
McTeague, Thomas **EGM**
Miles, Alfred **AM**
Miller, Thomas **EGM**
Mitchell, John **AM**
Morteshed, Francis **EGM**
Muhammad, Muhammad **EGM**
Naughton, Frank **EGM**
Newman, Alfred **AM**
Nix, Frank **EM**
Oliver, Dick **AM**
Orr, Samuel **EGM**
Parker, Edward **EGM**
Pearson, Robert **EM**
Pollitt, James **EM**
Rackham, Geoffrey **AM**
Reeves, James **AM**
Rhoades, William **AM**

Howarth, Albert **AM**
Humphreys, Patrick **EGM**
Hutchison, Albert **AM**
Jameson, Thomas **EM**
Johnston, James **EM**
Jones, Benjamin **EM**
Kelly, Cecil **EGM**
Keogh, Michael **AM**
King, Richard **EM**
Lee, Walter **EM**
Lloyd, William **EM**
Low, John **EGM**
Lungley, Alfred **EGM**
Mahoney, Herbert **EGM**
Manwaring, Thomas **EM**
Mata Din **EGM**
May, Phillip **AM**
McAvoy, Thomas **EGM**
McCabe, John **EM**
McClymont, John **EGM**
McKechnie, William **EGM**
Meadows, Albert **EM**
Miller, Henry **EGM**
Mirghany, Ahmed **EGM**
Morris, Alfred **EM**
Mott, Joseph **EGM**
Nandlal Thapa **EGM**
Negib, Ibrahim **EGM**
Niven, George **EGM**
O'Hagan, Leo **EGM**
Omara, Edwardo **EGM**
O'Shea, John **EGM**
Pearson, Joan **EGM**
Pir Khan **EGM**
Purvis, James **EM**
Rangit Singh **EGM**
Reynolds, Edward **EGM**
Richards, Richard **AM**

176

Ridling, Randolph AM
Rimmer, Reginald EGM
Robinson, Harry EM
Saunders, Robert EM
Sewell, Stanley EGM
Shepherd, John EM
Soulsby, Oliver EM
Stanners, John AM
Stoves, John EGM
Sylvester, William EGM
Talbot, Ellis EGM
Taylor, Patrick EGM
Thomas, Arthur EM
Thomas, Thomas EM
Tollemache, Anthony EGM
Troake, Frederick EGM
Tutton, Cyril EGM
Vaughan, Margaret AM
Walton, Eric AM
Waterfield, Albert EGM
Watson, Victor AM
Weller, Percy EM
Whitehead, Thomas EM
Wild, Robert EGM
Williams, Sidney AM
Wiltshire, Sidney EGM
Wolsey, Hilda AM
Yates, Philip EM
Young, Archibald EM

Riley, Geoffrey AM
Robertson, Paul AM
Rodrigues, George EGM
Schofield, Carl EM
Shanley, Joseph EM
Smith, Charles EM
Spoors, Robert AM
Stewart, James EGM
Sykes, Frank EM
Taha, El Jak EGM
Tandy-Green, Charles, EGM
Temperley, Samuel EM
Thomas, Dorothy EGM
Thompson, Matthew EM
Townsend, Emma EGM
Turner, James EGM
Tyler, Albert EM
Walker, Charles AM
Wastie, Granville EM
Waterson, William EM
Watt-Bonar, Eric EGM
Western, David AM
Wilcox, Charles EM
Williams, Osmond EM
Wilson, Harry EM
Winter, Gerald EGM
Yar, Ahmed EGM
Yehia, El Imam EGM
Younger, William EM

'I have just finished reading *Rounding the Horn* and have thoroughly enjoyed the whole aquatic adventure. Dallas Murphy is a master of the salty yarn. His history is spliced with a Roaring Forties imagination, and his passion for wild water infects every page with tremendous energy. This is both an evocation of extreme sailing, and a terrible, poignant account of two cultures clashing at the end of the earth. Murphy writes with compassion and verve of the nerve-wracking encounters between bewildered European sailors and the redoubtable tribes of Tierra del Fuego. Incomprehensible seas from *The Perfect Storm* share the pages with wave-lashed windjammers and doomed castaways. The author's decision to narrate the saga from the deck of a sailing yacht among the reefs and passages of the Horn, invests his book with compelling authenticity. As a reader, I found myself both appalled and fascinated by this most famous and savage of capes, and full of admiration for a writer who has succeeded in telling its story so convincingly'   Nicholas Crane, author of *Mercator*

'A delightful book that mixes history and travel. Murphy brings to life people, places and the past, exploring uncharted waters with Columbus, da Gama, Balboa and Magellan . . . I can't remember the last time I had so much fun reading, curling up comfortably for such an articulate adventure. Murphy's writing is vivid, his tales by turns admiring, irreverent, contemplative'   *Seattle Times*

'*Rounding the Horn* is an enthralling book that covers plenty of ground and water . . . Dallas Murphy writes with the authority of someone who has been to the places he describes . . . That point of view is especially agreeable when it results in a book as good as this one'   Norman Brown, Associated Press

'An enjoyable primer, compellingly salty in its retellings. As a bonus, Murphy's explanations of meteorology – such as the windy ambushings of the marvellously named williwaws – are among the clearest and most landlubber-friendly I've read . . . a highly readable and meticulously researched homage to the world's most ragged extremity'   Nick Thorpe, *Daily Telegraph*

Dallas Murphy is the author of several novels, including *Lush Life* and *Apparent Wind*, and the plays *The Terrorists* and *The Explorers*. His column on piloting and boating safety appears in *Offshore* magazine. Murphy, who lives in New York City, races one-designs (J-24s) on Long Island Sound and sails offshore, preferably to wild places, whenever possible.